NEW DIRECTIONS FOR HIGHER EDUCATION

Martin Kramer
*EDITOR-IN-CHIEF*

# Information Technology and the Remaking of the University Library

Beverly P. Lynch
*University of California, Los Angeles*

*EDITOR*

Number 90, Summer 1995

JOSSEY-BASS PUBLISHERS
San Francisco

INFORMATION TECHNOLOGY AND THE REMAKING OF THE
UNIVERSITY LIBRARY
*Beverly P. Lynch* (ed.)
New Directions for Higher Education, no. 90
Volume XXIII, Number 2
*Martin Kramer*, Editor-in-Chief

LC 85-644752          ISSN 0271-0560          ISBN 0-7879-9918-0

NEW DIRECTIONS FOR HIGHER EDUCATION is part of The Jossey-Bass
Higher and Adult Education Series and is published quarterly by Jossey-
Bass Inc., Publishers, 350 Sansome Street, San Francisco, California
94104-1342. Second-class postage paid at San Francisco, California, and
at additional mailing offices. POSTMASTER: Send address changes to New
Directions for Higher Education, Jossey-Bass Inc., Publishers, 350 Sansome Street, San Francisco, California 94104-1342.

SUBSCRIPTIONS for 1995 cost $48.00 for individuals and $64.00 for institutions, agencies, and libraries.

EDITORIAL CORRESPONDENCE should be sent to the Editor-in-Chief, Martin
Kramer, 2807 Shasta Road, Berkeley, California 94708-2011.

Cover photograph and random dot by Richard Blair/Color & Light © 1990.

TCF   Manufactured in the United States of America on Lyons Falls
      Pathfinder Tradebook. This paper is acid-free and 100 percent
totally chlorine-free.

# CONTENTS

# EDITOR'S NOTES

The last five years have brought great advances in the information technologies available to students and faculty in the nation's higher education institutions. As computer networks gained worldwide capabilities and information resources became available on-line and in digital format, people began to anticipate a revolutionary change in the instructional environments and sought to apply the technologies to teaching and learning. This volume explores some of the thinking about these issues from leaders in various sectors of American higher education. That a revolution has begun is generally agreed upon; what its immediate impact may be and what the future holds is neither agreed upon nor certain.

Institutions of higher education continue to change as new information technologies are adopted and applied to all aspects of academic life. Many of the changes are both obvious and expected. Higher education has embraced each new technological advance as it has appeared, particularly if it seems beneficial to the work of the faculty, students, and campus staff. The presence of on-line catalogs in the libraries and computers throughout the campus has been called the "modernization of the campus information infrastructure." Those in the academic community who bring about this modernization—and pay for it—are aware, of course, of the efforts needed to do so. But by and large these efforts are taken for granted; faculty, students, and staff simply use the technologies whenever it seems appropriate to do so in their work.

Another change of a more profound nature is also under way: the steady transformation of the printed record on which scholarly communication has been based and on which much of the instruction relies. More and more information is being created, stored, and delivered in digital formats. The move from printed to electronic form will influence every aspect of academic life. Libraries, which have had the responsibility of acquiring, organizing, providing access to, and preserving the scholarly record, are furnishing on-line information routinely, and campuses are building the infrastructure to enable access to the network environment. As the scholarly record changes, some unsettling trends are emerging with which the entire academic community must engage (Lynch, 1994). Some extraordinary opportunities also present themselves, however, and may affect higher education in very positive ways.

The purpose of this volume is to identify some of the trends being confronted as information technology becomes more pervasive. The authors present issues and concerns that the transformation will raise while campus administrators, faculty members, and others work to find ways to move easily and well to the new electronic environment.

The new technologies will enable the academic enterprise to be sustained and enhanced even while undergoing wrenching modification. Members of the academic community engaged in the transformation effort must continue to manage the current enterprise while positioning their institutions and the units within them to manage the effort. This is not easy in any period and is particularly difficult when the task is so revolutionary. It also is difficult for the faculty. Faculty must learn the new technology or be left behind by progress and the students who grew up with its convenience and availability.

This volume focuses on the units providing the information technology to the campus. In many respects the libraries and the agencies on campus that provide the necessary infrastructure are central to the continuing use and development of information technology. These agencies have responded quickly and well to the explosion of electronic information resources and the expansion of the Internet. The authors in this volume speak primarily about libraries because they view the library as a central component in the restructuring of teaching and learning; all assume that the technical infrastructure to enable access and use of the new technologies will be provided.

In Chapter One, Donald N. Langenberg offers a broad assessment of today's higher education environment. He describes the growing heterogeneity of the student body, which is a continuation of the historical trend toward expansion of access to higher education. A diversity of academic programs and a broader array of delivery modes and mechanisms are needed today. Langenberg anticipates that the developments in information technology will be central in meeting the demands of the new student body and of other challenges as well.

In Chapter Two, Richard M. Johnson discusses the political environment of the college campus. He describes the need for the library to position itself politically in order to place itself at the center of the decision-making structures. Johnson believes that the leaders in the support units that are heavily engaged in the development and the application of information technologies can position their units to achieve the vision of the future. Unlike those in the academic departments or colleges, the directors of these units are used to thinking of the campus as a whole. With that perspective and careful design, good results will be achieved. Although some have focused on the organizational arrangements of libraries and computer centers, the organizational structure is of less concern than the activities carried out to support instruction and research (Dougherty, 1995).

William Goodrich Jones emphasizes, in Chapter Three, the work of those scholars who use print and paper sources in their research, the humanists. Jones contrasts their work with that of scientists. He reminds us that the humanists form a central part of higher education. Although they are not as heavily funded as the scientists, their role cannot be overlooked. It sometimes is because they make few demands. Although they do not seek out the new technology, they use whatever is necessary for their work. Overall, the information technologies have had little influence on them so far. In terms of teaching, information technology, as it is changing the nature of authority, needs careful attention by these scholars and others (Lynch, 1994).

Some observers of the current environment have described a shift in the research library's mission from one that is "collection-based" to one that is "user-based." It should be acknowledged, as Jones and Ross Atkinson do in Chapters Three and Four, that the activities carried out in academic libraries for many years—building and maintaining collections, providing access to the collections, developing catalogs and bibliographical tools, and providing expert staff support—served library users in exactly the ways they wished. Faculty sought out institutions whose libraries contained the collections they needed. As the new technological developments emerge and users, particularly students, make greater use of on-line systems, librarians have begun to shift their mission from collections to access and to use, as Ralph A. Wolff explains in Chapter Six.

Atkinson states unequivocally that "without collections of some kind, information is useless." He offers an important perspective on the digital library and what it means for the academic enterprise. This is the central issue before the academy as rapid advances in information technology continue. Atkinson sees that in building on the past—on the analog environment as he calls it—a new library will emerge if the opportunity is seized to redesign all aspects of the scholarly information exchange.

In Chapter Five, Carla J. Stoffle and Karen Williams discuss the need to redesign the undergraduate educational program to emphasize learning. They present a model that integrates librarians into the teaching enterprise to help students gain the technological skills to become lifelong independent learners and in which learning outcomes are emphasized. The authors build on the bibliographical instruction model prevalent in academic libraries in the 1970s and 1980s, expanding it to offer a collaborative design in which librarians would work in teams with faculty. Bibliographic instruction programs were designed by librarians to systematically provide students with specific skills needed to complete course assignments. Students were instructed in the structure of information sources, how to access information sources, and how sources are physically organized. The most successful of these programs have been those that relate directly to a particular course assignment.

In Chapter Six, Wolff continues the discussion of learning and the assessment of educational outcomes. He considers the issue of appropriate quality indicators and states that "one important element of any self-study should be an exploration of the library's contribution to student learning." He carries the concept further to a rethinking of the library's purpose as information technologies expand, and then moves the library into a more central role: teacher to all within the academy. Wolff recognizes that libraries are connected to both the subject matter of learning and the emerging technologies for access.

In the concluding chapter, Clifford A. Lynch places the evolution of the library into the broader context of the forces shaping the university and altering the nature of the scholarly disciplines. Although the library has supported the teaching, research, and service missions of the university, it has operated autonomously. It has been able to do so because the campus mission has remained stable and well understood. But as the campus environment changes and information technologies continue to develop rapidly, library services and operations will be determined collaboratively in the context of the university's goals and mission.

The issues considered by the authors of this volume are central to the future of the college and university as we know them. To bring about the coming transformation, a solid understanding of the factors at play is required. The academic support units as we have known them, particularly the library, will play an increasingly important role in identifying the issues, investigating the policy implications and effects on instruction and research, and ensuring that information technology will indeed support the central purposes of teaching, research, and service.

Beverly P. Lynch
Editor

## References

Dougherty, R. M. "Repositioning of Campus Information Units for the Era of Digital Libraries." Unpublished manuscript, School of Information and Library Studies, University of Michigan, 1995.
Lynch, C. A. "Rethinking the Integrity of the Scholarly Record in the Networked Information Age." *Educom Review*, Mar.–Apr. 1994, *29*, 38–40.

*BEVERLY P. LYNCH is professor at the Graduate School of Education and Information Studies and former dean of the Graduate School of Library and Information Science, University of California, Los Angeles.*

*The rapidly changing environment of American colleges and universities portends major changes as information technology helps institutions respond.*

# The University and Information Technology: Interpreting the Omens

*Donald N. Langenberg*

The American higher education community is gradually gaining an unsettled awareness that something big is stirring in its midst. But what that something is is not yet clear. Is it a fierce monster from the deep? A hurricane from some Eastern shore? A tsunami induced by an unwitnessed earthquake under the sea? Or, rather, a gradual change due to a slow but inexorable rise in sea level caused by melting glaciers in some faraway polar sea?

Although the correct interpretation is not yet clear, the omens, as I call them, are plain to see for those who only look. Some are extensions of trends that began decades or even centuries ago. Others are of more recent origin. None come as a surprise. Nevertheless, such is our self-satisfaction at having built the biggest and best higher education enterprise in the history of the world that when it is suggested that the system has entered an extended period of profound change the response is often denial and disbelief. How can one imagine substantial change in so successful and important an enterprise?

Yet, judging from the trade journals of academe and, increasingly, the popular press, the voices of those prophesying change are increasing in both number and volume. Some—one might call them optimists—foresee a rosy future in which knowledge is widely acknowledged to be society's most valuable economic resource and in which the universities that dominate the pinnacle of the knowledge pyramid become richer and even more important with the aid of the new information technology. Others—call them pessimists—foresee the impending demise of all that university scholars have labored to create within the ivy-covered halls of learning.

Whatever one's position, it is hard not to suspect that where there is so much talk there must be substance, perhaps even something worthy of

NEW DIRECTIONS FOR HIGHER EDUCATION, no. 90, Summer 1995 © Jossey-Bass Publishers

attention. So, for the moment, let us suspend whatever disbelief we may have and examine the omens. Then I hope the reader will consider my speculations about their meaning and what we ought to do about them.

## The Omen of Student Heterogeneity

For centuries, the student bodies of Western universities were homogeneous. They were made up of the young sons of wealthy families who were being groomed for leadership roles in the church, the government, or other institutions of society. Whatever their national homeland, the students shared the universal language of instruction—Latin—and many other cultural attributes. There was general agreement that the proper curriculum for them should be founded on the unchanging historical legacy of Western thought and its pillars of theology, law, and the classical tradition.

Then, in the mid-eighteenth century, Benjamin Franklin and others advocated adding to the curriculum subjects of a more practical nature, such as mathematics and "natural philosophy," as the sciences were then termed. These were believed to be of utility to young gentlemen who would be called upon to oversee enterprises requiring more than traditional concepts and methods. As the industrial revolution gained momentum, the importance of such subjects became more widely recognized. The value to society of extending access to higher education to students from a wider range of backgrounds also became evident. In the United States this led to the passage of the Morrill Act of 1862 and the development of universities intended to train "the children of the industrial class" in the skills required for the new "agriculture and mechanic arts." In these universities the sons of the industrial class soon found themselves studying side by side with the sons of the ruling class.

Also in the nineteenth century the sons of all classes began to find themselves studying with the daughters as society's leaders realized that there was value in educating women. At first this was done apart; institutions created for women alone avoided compromising both the young men's education and the young women's virtue. Eventually it was discovered that men and women could be educated together without harming either.

During the same period, institutions dedicated to the higher education of African Americans began to appear. Like the early women's colleges, these institutions were separated from the established institutions although for different reasons. It took much longer (a century) before we understood and acknowledged that whatever the advantages of single-sex or single-race institutions a democratic society must provide its citizens higher education opportunities that are unconditioned by gender or race.

Thus, in the nineteenth century and particularly in the United States, the student population's characteristics with respect to gender, race, and socioeconomic status began to evolve toward the corresponding characteristics of the general population. This evolution quickened considerably in the twentieth century with the G.I. Bill, the civil rights movement, and a growing national prosperity that opened the way to higher education for a substantial portion of the population. It continues today and has by no means reached its end point.

In recent decades our student population began to diversify along yet another dimension, age. The trend has been driven by the evolution of the U.S. economy toward one in which knowledge and knowledge-based skills have increasingly displaced physical labor and the exploitation of natural resources as the essential ingredients of productivity and economic success. The pace of this displacement has become so rapid that the nature of these essential ingredients now changes substantially in a short time compared with the length of a working career. Consequently, a greater proportion of the population needs higher education and, at the same time, it is increasingly difficult to acquire all the knowledge and skills needed for a lifetime of work in the brief period of a few years at college. Consequently, we are seeing growing participation of older adults in conventional university programs and significant growth in unconventional university programs designed to provide continuing education for adults of all ages. One of the institutions of the University of Maryland System recently reported that the ages of the members of its incoming freshman class ranged from fifteen to seventy-two. It has been estimated that close to half of all American university and college undergraduates are now twenty-five years of age or older.

## The Omen of Consumerism

When higher education was a relatively simple product consumed by a limited and well-heeled clientele, its price was not an issue. That is no longer the case. Opinion polls today consistently show that the public views higher education as essential to its well-being, a necessity rather than a luxury. The public also expresses strong concern that the price of higher education threatens to become unacceptably high.

Accompanying concern about price is a growing concern about the quality and value of higher education. If higher education is both essential and costly then it is important to be sure that it offers value and meets the consumer's needs. This implies that the providers of higher education must demonstrate the quality and value of their product by finding ways to measure and characterize the quality and value in a manner that their clients find understandable and persuasive. It will no longer do to say simply, "Trust us. We're the experts and we know what we're doing. You're getting exactly what you need."

The increasing heterogeneity of our student body brings with it demands for a greater diversity of academic programs and a broader array of delivery modes and mechanisms. Within academe, this trend is sometimes oversimplified and decried as a movement toward narrow vocationalism and away from the time-honored values of a broad liberal education. Such an attitude is unfortunate and trivializes a fundamental aspect of higher education's role in modern society. The importance of liberal education has certainly not declined but increased as the events and trends that affect people's lives have expanded from local to national to global and encompassed an enormous array of social, political, economic, and technological developments. But the emergence of the knowledge-based economy also means that the economic well-being of most people depends on their ability to develop and maintain sophisticated practical skills that once were the province of society's elite. If this is "vocationalism" then it is a central aspect of life today, not a regrettable symptom of decline from a golden past. We must understand it and respond to it. Higher education must continue to provide a balanced blend of liberal education and vocational skills suited to the varying needs of its varied clients.

Our heterogeneous student clientele also includes a growing number of people for whom traditional delivery modes and mechanisms are inadequate and inappropriate. An example is the adult student who cannot travel far because of work or home location and responsibilities but who seeks new knowledge and skills for personal advancement or to enhance quality of life. Such students frequently lack easy access to a campus or the ability to attend classes at conventional times. They are no longer a small minority; they constitute close to half of all American college and university students. They often want new knowledge in areas in which their own practical experience far exceeds that of most faculty. The motivations and expectations of these students differ significantly from those of traditional students. For such students, different—sometimes radically different—means for meeting educational needs are called for.

Finally, indicative of the new consumerism is an increasingly common expectation that higher education be "hassle-free." This is not an expectation that learning be made easy but that the learning environment be freed of unnecessary and counterproductive impediments. Students want administrative services that are not bureaucratic nightmares. They want close and effective contacts with faculty. They want to be informed about issues that matter to them. They want institutions to treat them like valued clients. There was a time when higher education was a commodity in short supply and its few consumers were compelled to accept it on its own terms. That time has passed. The number and variety of providers of higher education have increased and continue to increase. We are moving from an era of "father knows best" to one of "the customer is always right." Other providers of goods and services have experienced such changes. It now seems to be higher education's turn. And that observation brings us to the next omen.

## The Omen of Competition

Our colleges and universities are accustomed to thinking of themselves as the only significant providers of postsecondary education. Although they have competed with one another, the notion of alternative opportunities for postsecondary education has been foreign to them. But evidence that this attitude may require some adjustment is appearing. The most obvious indication is that competition among colleges and universities is growing fiercer. There is movement of students from private institutions to public institutions, from four-year schools to community colleges, and from public institutions in one state to those in others.

At the same time, other competitors are beginning to appear. Business firms have long been in the business of training their own employees. The magnitude of this sector of postsecondary education is widely underappreciated; it is estimated that total expenditures by American businesses for employee training exceed total expenditures by American colleges and universities. One hears not infrequently from business leaders that they find it necessary to make up for deficiencies in their college graduate employees' preparation through on-the-job training. Of course, much of this training can appropriately be described as narrowly focused vocational training, but not all of it can. Some of it looks for all the world like what colleges and universities provide. In an increasingly competitive world, it is not unreasonable to wonder whether businesses that have learned how to educate their own employees effectively and efficiently might not decide that there is money to be made by applying their expertise more generally.

One particularly notable such business is the information industry. (This industry represents an important omen in itself, about which more follows in a later section of this chapter.) For some time, decades at least, publishers of books and journals and providers of communication services (for example, mail and telecommunication systems) and information processing machinery (for example, computers) have been the source of key tools for the education industry (that is, colleges and universities). We are now witnessing the convergence of these enterprises in an information industry that finds itself with the capability to move beyond merely supplying tools to the actual provision of some forms of education. This fact has not escaped some industry leaders. What they might do remains to be seen but it would be foolish to discount this potential source of competition.

Two observations may illustrate the point. First, the traditional means of teaching a child to play the piano is to hire a piano teacher. But recently a multimedia computer software product has appeared that reportedly does a very adequate job of introductory piano instruction. The cost: less than a hundred dollars. Second, Bill Gates, the CEO of Microsoft Corporation, has publicly expressed interest in the "education market." It is noteworthy that Mr. Gates' personal fortune reportedly exceeds the total endowment of the nation's richest university.

## The Omen of Limited Resources

The observation that the financial and human resources available to colleges and universities are limited is not new, it is an eternal reality. What is new, however, is the concurrent limitations now placed on the various sources of revenue upon which our institutions depend. Few of today's academics ever experienced a time when there was little prospect that new initiatives could be supported through increased funding from one source or another. We now find ourselves in such a time. Both public and private institutions are meeting resistance to tuition increases following a decade or more of increases at rates well above the growth rates of family income and consumer prices. Struggling state economies and growing popular demands for containing or reducing taxes and for shrinking government have led to tightly constrained or substantially reduced state funding for public institutions. Federal support for student financial aid and research and development appears vulnerable to sudden shifts and, perhaps, decreases. Private donations to colleges and universities remain robust but our donors' pockets are not infinitely deep while donors are sought ever more aggressively by ever more institutions. And all of this is occurring in a tumultuous environment: our national economy appears to be in a fragile state of reasonably good health but the country's ability to continue to prosper in an increasingly competitive and turbulent global economy remains a concern. As a result, the traditional academic argument—that we have important things to do and should therefore be given more money to do them—is now commonly met with the response, "We have more pressing problems. You'll be lucky to keep what you have."

## The Omen of Information Technology

We are currently witnessing the near-explosive emergence of an epochal new technology—information technology. It has been a long time coming. The scientific understanding of electromagnetism in the late nineteenth century gave rise to several successive generations of telecommunication technologies beginning with the telegraph and the telephone and progressing to radio and television. In the mid-twentieth century the programmable digital computer appeared. In several generations that device has evolved from a specialized tool for the few to a ubiquitous staple of everyday life. Over the past couple of decades these telecommunication and computer technologies have married and produced a powerful offspring, information technology. Many of us have yet to find the on-ramp to the information superhighway but the number of us who find the very notion irrelevant is dwindling rapidly.

Although information technology has some of its roots in the research laboratories of our universities and has been exploited since its earliest days by university scientists, it is only gradually becoming evident that it has profound implications for all of education. It is not hard to understand why. Information is the building block of education. From it we synthesize knowledge that we store and convey to our colleagues and students in the hope of generating understanding and perhaps even wisdom. Any technology that revolutionizes our capabilities for creating, manipulating, storing, and transmitting information must necessarily revolutionize our educational enterprise. The nature and extent of this revolution has yet to be fully revealed but many assert that nothing about our academic processes or institutions can long remain untouched by it. Lanham (1993), for example, has argued persuasively that information technology will change the very way we think and will call into question the continued existence of such academic mainstays as the lecture, the class, the library, even the campus itself.

For the skeptical academic who finds such assertions to be just so much hyperbole, it may be useful to cite an earlier example of the powerful impact of a new information technology on the work of an academic and on the lives of his contemporaries and successors. One day in 1517, a professor at the University of Wittenberg posted a notice on the door of the university chapel inviting his colleagues to a public debate of some ninety-five propositions. (Professors found it difficult even then to be brief.) Had this notice not been reproduced with a recently developed information technology called printing, and had it not been disseminated on the medieval equivalent of the Internet, the debate might have passed with little notice or effect. Instead, Professor Luther became the founder of a new church, gave the impetus for the Thirty Years War, and began the political transformation of Europe. To be sure, it was his ideas and not the technology that really caused the ruckus. But had there been no printing press in Wittenberg it seems likely Luther would have ended his days as little more than a harmless academic crank.

## Interpreting the Omens—and Acting

What do these omens portend? In a word, change! Rapid change. Revolutionary change. Unprecedented change.

Of course, our colleges and universities have changed in the past. They have changed steadily, repeatedly, and, at times, abruptly. They have adapted to the transformation of their student clientele from a small homogeneous elite to a cross section of a diverse population and in the process they have proliferated in number and kind and grown enormously in size, wealth, and importance. They have added the role of creators of knowledge to their ancient roles of custodians and purveyors of knowledge. They have responded to changing markets and growing consumerism by adding to their liberal arts and science cores a tremendous variety of professional and vocational programs. They have maintained and enhanced their competitive positions in the face of competition from other types of educational enterprises, both domestic and international. In short, they have changed and adapted so well that they may be said to be among our nation's most successful institutional inventions.

So what is so different about the present moment in our history? Why should we suppose that anything other than the familiar agents and mechanisms of academic change are required? In my opinion, the reasons are to be found in the simultaneous accelerating growth of *all* of the trends discussed so far in this chapter. We might have been able to respond to any one of them alone through traditional means but because they are all hitting at the same time, an extraordinary response is required. It is our good fortune that the last trend—information technology—is emerging just when we need an extraordinary tool with which to make that extraordinary response. Information technology is not in and of itself the solution to our problems but it has the potential to make a solution feasible if we can muster the creativity, courage, and will necessary to deal with them.

Where to begin? I think we must begin by acknowledging that we will have to accomplish rapid and significant change without the customary incentive of new funds for new initiatives. The necessary change will of course frequently require up-front investment. In some institutions new funds may sometimes be available but we should expect that in many instances we will have to reallocate funds from existing applications. This is something we are not used to doing in academe. It is a fertile source of controversy and conflict in a culture where collegial debate leading (sometimes) to consensus is often preferred over strategic design and decisive action. And it will be painful. In such circumstances, the path of least resistance is to eschew new initiatives and the investment decisions they require. Although many will choose that path, I believe that institutions that take the more difficult path of reallocation and reinvestment for change will enhance their probability of success in the new environment.

As we confront these difficult choices we can expect advice from outside academe, including some unwelcome prodding and even attempts at micromanagement. Parents, alumni, the business community, and politicians and pundits of all kinds are becoming considerably more vocal in expressing their perceptions of our shortcomings and what we should do about them. They are asking hard questions about the unresponsiveness, ineffectiveness, and inefficiencies of our bureaucracies, about the ways in which we govern ourselves and allocate our human and financial resources among our multiple functions, and about our institutional priorities. Faculty workload and responsibilities and the balance between teaching and research have become subjects for political debate in many states. The institution of tenure appears likely to come under close scrutiny before long.

An honest evaluation of this situation suggests that it is not as bad as we may sometimes pretend. We are not really under serious attack. We are simply being forced to reexamine and reevaluate aspects of our higher education enterprise that we ourselves should long ago have taken the initiative to review and, where necessary, adjust. As long as the outcome of this review is not preordained by its extramural initiators, it can be a very healthy thing. However, we must try to avoid the imposition of damaging answers to appropriate and helpful questions.

As we grapple with the question of how to create necessary change within stringent resource constraints, the most obvious and recurrent answer is that we simply increase our productivity. Dramatic productivity increases have been key to the survival and continuing success of many American industries, including some (like the steel industry) once thought to be in terminal decline. Our critics and our friends say, "If they can do it, why can't higher education?"

Unfortunately, the knee-jerk reaction of academe to that question is, too often, to take umbrage. We often assert huffily that teaching and research are arts of the highest order, not mere mechanical processes, and that it is thus ludicrous to attempt to improve productivity. The point is sometimes made by using some form of the "Mozart Argument," that is, by noting that the performance of a Mozart symphony today requires the same number of musicians playing for the same amount of time as was required in Mozart's time. Thus, just as no improvement in the production efficiency of a Mozart symphony performance has occurred in two centuries, no improvement in the production efficiency of a college or university can reasonably be expected.

But closer examination of this argument reveals that it contains some flaws. First, it is presented from the point of view of the orchestra members, that is, the performers. It is true that, from their point of view, the process of performing a Mozart symphony hasn't changed much in two hundred years. But is that the appropriate point of view? Does the orchestra exist for the enjoyment (and employment) of its members? Of course not! It exists for the purpose of providing high-quality musical experiences for its listeners. If the Mozart symphony business is examined from their point of view it quickly becomes apparent that its productivity has increased dramatically since Mozart's day. Of course, if the listener is fortunate enough to have access to a symphony orchestra and attends a performance, that performance will proceed in much the same way. But if the listener is not so blessed, or if he or she simply prefers to hear another program or even another orchestra, slipping the appropriate CD into the living room sound system will satisfy those desires nicely, conveniently, and inexpensively. From the listener's point of view technology has obviously had a great deal to do with improved productivity of this artistic business.

Pursuing the analogy, I believe that we academics too often think and behave as if our institutions exist primarily for our own enjoyment and employment. Unfortunately, doing so leads us astray when we think about the future. We would do better to look into our institutions' futures from the viewpoints of our clientele rather than of our faculty and staff. In this way it should be easier to spot and avoid such "traps" as the conclusion that no productivity increases are possible. Fortunately, the notion that productivity increases *can* be achieved in colleges and universities—and that they must be—is spreading across the academic landscape.

One of the influential sources of this idea is the Pew Higher Education Research Program. In *Policy Perspectives,* it puts it this way: "Given strong leadership and a sustained commitment to the retraining of current staff, we believe that a five- to seven-year process designed to reengineer operations can yield a 25 percent reduction in the number of full-time employees an institution requires" (Pew Higher Education Research Program, 1993).

Putting it this way tends to create visions of layoffs in the minds of employees and thus derail further constructive thought about how such a reduction might be realized. It also reflects an implicit assumption that at the end of the five-to-seven year process the institution will continue to serve the same clientele at the same level of quality but with fewer employees. Many institutions now face increasing enrollment and other changing demands that invalidate this assumption.

A more palatable and applicable form of the Pew goal statement would be the following: "Given strong leadership and a sustained commitment to retraining, we believe that a five- to seven-year process designed to reengineer operations can yield a 25 percent increase in the productivity of our institutions." The reader will have noticed that the original Pew form actually corresponds to a 33 percent increase in productivity for those remaining employees. We have chosen to be a tad less ambitious.

What would be required for a college or university actually to achieve this goal? First, it would have to figure out exactly what productivity means in such an institution. It has often been remarked that the higher education industry may be the only industry that cannot define the nature and quantity of its own products well enough to provide a plausible estimate of its productivity. Although something of an exaggeration, there is considerable truth in the statement. Admittedly, the issue is complex, involving both qualitative and quantitative factors. But it is one we need to take up before others do it for us. We need to understand how to move away from input indicators like dollars spent, books owned, and credit hours earned, to true output indicators. We need to understand how to accommodate the effects of differences between disciplines and institution types. And because interinstitutional and intrainstitutional comparisons are both useful and inevitable, we must seek to develop common measures and standards we all can use.

While we are trying to figure out what productivity means, we must also get down to the business of increasing it. At first it will be easier to see how to do that on the administrative side than on the academic side. The administrative support elements of a college or university closely resemble corresponding elements in many other service industries. Examples of productivity enhancement in service industries are growing in number. They generally involve reengineering administrative processes to simplify them, placing responsibility for their implementation in the hands of fewer people with broader responsibilities, flattening administrative hierarchies, loosening the lines connecting the boxes on the institutional organization chart, and blurring the lines around the boxes. In many cases, this is facilitated or even made possible by substantial strengthening of the information technology infrastructure that supports administrative services.

It will be more difficult to learn how to achieve large productivity increases on the academic side and it will take longer to do so but the potential rewards are greater. What is involved is a thoroughgoing transformation of what faculty do and how they do it, aided and abetted by a massive infusion of the new information technology into the teaching and learning enterprise. Lanham (1993) and others have adumbrated the radical nature of this coming transformation. The technology will change the way we think, teach, and learn.

The nature of the change is suggested by a topological analogy. Let's think of the learning environment transformed from a one-dimensional thing (such as a string) to a two-dimensional thing (such as the surface of a sphere). In the one-dimensional environment, the learning process has a beginning and an end, and everything about it, from textbooks to courses, is made compatible with a serial process through which learners progress. In the more complex environment of the new information technology, learning is a multidimensional (and multimedia) process with no fixed beginning or end and many paths leading to a goal. The surface of a sphere has no beginning and no end and no middle and no edges; it offers infinite ways to get from one point to another on the surface.

The balance of faculty functions will shift from the present emphasis on conveying knowledge through lectures to guiding and mentoring students as they navigate among information systems and sources along paths tailored to meet their individual needs. Those information systems and sources may be designed and created by faculty, just as faculty now design and create textbooks. The mix of faculty talents needed may thus come to resemble those required to produce a movie or a television show. There would be faculty actors and actresses, among them a few famous stars. There would be faculty producers and directors, screenwriters, and stuntpeople. As for the colleges and universities that now are the faculty's institutional homes, the movie industry may similarly provide a helpful analogy. At one time, large studios employed numerous actors and actresses for whose services the studios competed with one another. The studios also employed directors and all the other specialists and experts needed to create the movies that were produced and distributed. But such studios no longer exist. Moviemakers and actors now function more independently, capitalizing on their reputations and applying their talents in a fluid and flexible market that includes production organizations that bear little resemblance to the old studios. Might not some of our universities go the way of MGM?

It is possible too that the information systems and sources that will provide the basic tools for tomorrow's higher education enterprise will not be designed by faculty as we now conceive of it. Instead they may be created by entrepreneurial scholars who operate in institutional environments that resemble television studios or software companies more than universities. Or the tools may come out of partnerships between traditional universities and other organization types. What would happen if Microsoft and Harvard merged?

There is no guarantee that productivity gains will be made from all this. But enough concrete examples are emerging from our universities showing what can be done with information technology to make it clear that higher education is on the verge of substantial change, that the professional lives of the next generation of faculty may not greatly resemble those of the present generation, and that American higher education can be transformed without a flood of new money.

If some combination of smarts, guts, and technology can enable a university (or a group of universities) to maneuver toward change within tight financial constraints then the same combination will help it deal with the consequences of the omens described in this chapter. The new information technology is just what the doctor ordered to help us deal with growing student heterogeneity, for example. To do so we must tailor our educational programs to a broad array of students wherever and whenever they wish to be reached. If we are to do this without sacrificing quality or access, we must find ways to combine the best features of an intimate teacher-student relationship with mass delivery of information, thus achieving what the auto industry calls *mass customization*.

Mass customization requires a degree of flexibility and adaptability that has been rare in academe. We are notorious for the rigidity and impermeability of the walls between our various units of academic "turf," our laboratories, centers, departments, schools, colleges, and universities. We will have to learn that there is power and value in a capacity to link and combine our resources in various (often transient) ways to meet a great variety of demands. Today's information technology provides both a model and a name for such an environment. It is a *client-server environment,* a networked array of processor units that can be applied either individually or collectively to meet a need in a manner tailored to the nature of the need. (The term also indicates the true object of the process—the client!)

If we can come to see our institutions as client-server systems and make them function in the manner suggested by their networked computer analogs, we will have gone a long way toward preparing them to meet the challenges they face. This notion may be useful at several organizational levels. It is easy to imagine several faculty members from different fields joining to develop a multimedia vehicle for delivering an interdisciplinary course on environmental science and policy. Equally easy to imagine are several universities cooperating in a similar endeavor. With a little more effort, we might imagine a client-server team that includes some nonacademic members (as, for example, in the Microsoft-Harvard merger idea already mentioned). The systems of colleges and universities that have become the mode of public higher education organization in the United States are naturals for becoming client-server systems. I am trying to encourage the institutions of my own system, the University of Maryland System, to think and behave in such a way and have met with more success than I had any reason to expect.

Innumerable applications of information technology can help colleges and universities respond to growing consumerism. Known examples range from relatively straightforward automation of existing functions, such as managing library collections, to prototypes for transforming specific courses from the old lecture mode to something very different and more student-friendly. Unknown examples remain just that—unknown. In one way or another, all have the effect of making the relationship between a university's clients—especially the students—much more efficient and serviceable and at the same time more intimate and human. The latter is not what the technophobes expect, but it is what technology can do if wisely applied.

What of the increasing competition? For the organization with a clear vision of its future and an idea of how to realize it, information technology provides an essential tool. It is a tool that is available to all of the organization's competitors, however, which may include similar organizations (its traditional competitors) and nontraditional and perhaps unexpected competitors. This is important for colleges and universities to understand. Something akin to deregulation of the airline or telecommunication industries is happening in the higher education industry. It is by no means certain that the industry leaders of the future will look like those of the past. It is not written anywhere that the apex of American higher education will always be associated with the brand names that once were the surnames of New England gentlemen or western railroad barons. It is not even written that that apex will continue to be occupied by colleges and universities.

The rules of the game are changing. Those who would continue to play must grasp the tools of the future and turn to the task of writing the game's new rules. The following chapters in this volume will give the reader a glimpse of what must be done. Let us get on with it.

## References

Lanham, R. A. *The Electronic Word: Democracy, Technology, and the Arts.* Chicago: University of Chicago Press, 1993.

Pew Higher Education Research Program. *Policy Perspectives,* 1993, 4 (4), 7A.

DONALD N. LANGENBERG *is chancellor of the University of Maryland System.*

*For libraries to continue to play important roles in the intellectual life of tomorrow's campus, they will have to position themselves politically as well as technologically.*

# New Technologies, Old Politics: Political Dimensions in the Management of Academic Support Services

*Richard M. Johnson*

College and university libraries are in the midst of reconsidering their very essence and their future. It may be said that the library has become a focal point for consideration of how academic institutions should be restructured for the challenges of the twenty-first century. There are plenty of other actors both within the academy and without who are thinking about the role and place of the academic library in the next century. Both "library as place" and the role of the librarian in an era of rapid change in the informational arena are being questioned.

The technological revolution has already had profound effects on the way services are offered to faculty and students, who are the primary "consumers" of academic library services. For better or for worse, card catalogues have become a thing of the past, replaced by on-line data bases. Bibliographic searches can now be done at remote terminals at several locations on campus or even in the comfort of one's own home. The treasured library, center of the traditional campus, is becoming a place that no longer has to be visited on a regular basis.

However, not only "library as place" is being questioned. Also being questioned is "college as place." For example, Arthur Levine, president of Columbia University Teachers College, foresees the decline of the traditional campus by the year 2050. He recently told Reuters: "What I'm expecting is, by the middle part of next century, there will be liberal arts colleges and research universities." Expensive, traditional liberal arts colleges, as he sees it, will be there for wealthy students who want a traditional education; other students will attend college electronically through personal computers. Levine points to changes in higher education behavior that have already taken place. Fewer than one-fifth of college students now live in traditional dormitories.

He cites the changing demographics of the college population and their patterns of behavior. Many are older. They work and have families and lives off campus. College is just one of many activities pursued. What students now want from a college is "good instruction, great service, low cost and convenience." These can be provided electronically to remote sites. Levine poses the question, "If you can do these things from your desk, why do you need a physical plant called a college?" ("In 2050, Computer May Be Collegian's 'Campus,'" 1994).

Colleges and universities across the land are engaged in strategic planning exercises that attempt to address these changes in technology and associated human behavior. In the development of these plans, academic support services—most centrally, the library and academic computer centers—will be a crucial battleground upon which the development of the university of the twenty-first century will be fought.

## Assumptions

My crystal ball does not tell me exactly how the important questions about the college or university of the twenty-first century will ultimately be decided. Although I agree that significant changes will be made in the way they conduct their business, primarily because of the advance of information technology and the costs associated with the maintenance of traditional academic services, I am unwilling to agree totally with Levine's assessment. I am at heart an academic traditionalist and one at the later stages of a long academic career that has included extensive faculty governance involvement and academic administrative service. I am unable to accept blithely the total demise of the traditional academic institution that I have been a part of for more than two-thirds of my life. I can, however, make certain assumptions about the nature of change that will occur over the next several years. I believe that the college and university of the twenty-first century will differ in operation from the academic institution of before in the following fundamental ways:

The advance of information technology will profoundly affect not only the delivery of knowledge to students but also the way in which knowledge is acquired and disseminated.

The new information technology will require fundamental changes in how the professorate is trained to carry out its instructional and research responsibilities and in how nonfaculty personnel are trained to carry out their support mission.

Rather than coming from "visionary" presidential leadership, what the college or university of the twenty-first century becomes will be the product of an interplay of political forces emanating from within the institution as well as without.

The college or university of the twenty-first century will be developed not with the aid of additional funding but in an environment of limited resources.

For simplicity and economy in presentation, in the following discussion I refer only to "the university" with the understanding that the discussion equally applies to the freestanding college.

## The Politics of Institutional Change

As a political scientist who has observed firsthand and participated intensively in various dimensions of university politics, I find it useful and appropriate to view the university as a political system, one in which identifiable stakeholders pursue what they perceive to be their vital self-interests. The stakeholders are not all contained within the organization itself; significant actors in the surrounding environment pursue their interests and play a large role in determining what goes on within the institution. Ultimately, decisions concerning the shape of the university of the twenty-first century will be the result of the interplay of the political forces both inside and outside the university. Let us first discuss the relevant external environment.

**External Factors.**  The impact of the revolution in information technology on the university of today and tomorrow has already been mentioned in this chapter. The traditional large lecture approach is particularly vulnerable as electronic means through television and computers become more effective and cost-beneficial in disseminating knowledge to large numbers of people both on and off the campus. As a major information-disseminating enterprise, the university cannot long afford to ignore the technological advances being made and must adapt to them.

The second important feature of the external environment is the limited availability of resources. The university of the late twentieth century is seen as only one of many institutions vying for a share of limited resources. Today's university is not seen to be sacrosanct, precious, and isolated, or something that should be accorded special status and preferential treatment.

Searching questions about the nature of the university are being raised within it by members of the academy, as the earlier quote from Arthur Levine attests. They are also being raised by boards of regents and other governing bodies who are seeking more direct involvement in the management of the enterprise. Such questioning fuels the wider public debate taking place where many of the folkways of the university are coming under close and often skeptical scrutiny. They ask the following kinds of questions about the professorate: Why does the faculty enjoy lifetime job security through tenure? Why do they work but six or eight hours per week? Why do they work only three-quarters of the year and still draw enormous salaries? They ask questions about the administrators: Why are there so many of them and why are they paid so well? They ask about the physical facilities: Why are the classrooms used for such a few hours per day and stand vacant during a good part of the year? As for the library, the list of skeptical questions is daunting: Why do they spend so much money for materials that seldom leave the shelves? Can we afford to continue to deal with the accelerated deterioration of our books? Aren't books obsolete anyway with the advent of the electronic revolution? And in general, they ask: Why shouldn't universities be run more like businesses?

Many of these questions are indicative of a broader crisis of public confidence with which universities must deal. This is encompassed within the PROF-SCAM (Sykes, 1990) mentality that delights in pointing out certain excesses in professorial behavior on university campuses. Another element is a part of the "Generation X" phenomenon. The contemporary university is not seen to be the engine for social mobility it once was. For a Generation X student a college degree, although still a valued commodity, does not guarantee that he or she will ultimately be economically better off than his or her parents.

The questions that are being raised, whether overtly economic in nature or not, have profound implications for the economics of higher education. They go to the very core of the academic enterprise and provide the context for critical self-examination in both public and private institutions nationwide. There is general recognition that universities cannot do and be all things to all people. In the public realm, state governing and coordinating boards are forcing institutions under their purview to identify and eliminate programs of low priority in order to shift resources to areas of higher priority. "Accountability," "productivity," "cost effectiveness," and "strategic planning" are the new watchwords being used while techniques of corporate management are being applied to the "business" of higher education.

Private and public institutions alike are finding that money problems cannot be handled by simply raising tuition. Publics and privates are becoming much more alike in their search for private funds. Universities of all kinds have embarked on significant capital fund drives, many of them in the range of hundreds of millions of dollars, some now even in the billions. The institutional development officer has thus assumed an increasingly important role in university decision-making councils.

In many respects, the fences between the academy and various external forces have eroded. Universities have become more like their corporate counterparts as the outside world has moved in on them. The imagery of the CEO and COO has infected the upper reaches of university administration. University administrators now often carry very corporate-sounding titles: there are executive associate vice-chancellors and executive associate deans; department heads and chairs are referred to as department executive officers. On campuses, individual entrepreneurial activity is recognized and rewarded. The phrase "every tub on its own bottom" signifies that deans are expected to generate funds to support the independent operation of their colleges. Independent entrepreneurial activity on the part of individual faculty members is similarly expected and rewarded.

As the demarcation between the academy and its environment blurs we must consider the related costs and benefits. There are surely both. Regardless of how one feels about this issue, it is clear that the environmental situation and its transactions with the university powerfully affect the political dynamics internal to the university.

**Internal Politics.** In many respects, what a university is depends on the pictures of the enterprise that one carries in one's head. Three sets of "pictures"—or more scientifically, models—are often used to depict the university or its parts. They play an important role in internal university politics (Baldridge and others, 1977). The three model types are bureaucratic, collegiate, and political.

The *bureaucratic model,* inspired by Max Weber, emphasizes legal rationality and bureaucratic hierarchy. It includes formal chains of command and systems of communication, a "rational" mode of decision making. This perspective "fits" fairly well the administrative side of the university because it captures the orientation of many support personnel. Most aspects of administration can be understood by using this model. Campus level administrators find it comfortable and convenient to view things from this perspective but often find that much of the university does not conform to this view.

The *collegiate model,* which differentiates the university from most other kinds of formal organizations, emphasizes the importance of a community of scholars, one in which the faculty plays a significant role in decision making and even management of the university. The elements of this perspective are reflected in the various structures of the university: departments, colleges, and the faculty senate. Decisions are the products of deliberation and reasoned debate. Obviously, many in the faculty see the university in this manner. The degree to which this model continues to be effective in the late twentieth century university is a matter of conjecture.

The *political model* places less emphasis on formal structure and procedure than the bureaucratic model does and emphasizes conflict instead of consensus as the collegiate model does. The focus is on decision making. Some of the key questions asked are the following: Who are the players? What resources do they bring to the table? What tactics do they employ? The emphasis is on bargaining and negotiation, with a decision being the outcome of a political process.

The political model does not supplant the other models but draws upon them and integrates them. For most routine decision making, the bureaucratic model is perfectly appropriate because, as with any organization, most decisions are routine. However, what differentiates routine from critical decision making is a key political question. Structure and formal organizational relations are important. As noted above, one whole side of the university dwells on "rational decision making," and the university leader's political position is enhanced by his or her formal position.

The collegiate model taps primitive feelings about what an academic institution is all about. At base, it is a normative model that characterizes how decision making should be carried out and who should be involved. The common distinction between academic and other administrators should be noted.

Although the former carry administrative responsibilities, because of the laws of the collegium they must generally hold tenure and highest professorial rank.

**Stakeholders.** The university may be seen as a political system made up of diverse forces, both internal and external, interacting to make decisions. Focusing internally on the academic enterprise, the key identifiable forces are the campus academic administrators (including chancellors or presidents, provosts, deans, and so on), other academic administrative leaders (directors of the library, computer center, and other academic support units), the faculty, academic support personnel, and the students. In order to explain more fully the political dynamics of the management of academic support services, it is necessary to examine these actors' roles.

*Campus Academic Administrators.* Campus academic administrators, and principally the chancellor or the president, speak from a campus orientation. They set and articulate campus goals and objectives, attempting to move the campus forward through the development of mission statements and other long-range planning documents. They are principally responsible for linking the university to the larger environment. They respond for the institution to coordinating and governing boards, political forces, and the community. They belong to various national academic administrative leadership organizations, such as the American Council of Education and the National Association of State Universities and Land Grant Colleges, which are sources of new ideas. They read the *Chronicle of Higher Education* to gain the wisdom of leaders like Ernest Boyer, president of the Carnegie Foundation for the Advancement of Teaching, who recently spelled out his views on creating the new American college (Boyer, 1994).

Boyer has called for the "'New American College,' an institution that celebrates teaching and selectively supports research while also taking special pride in its capacity to connect thought to action, theory to practice. . . . [One] committed to improving, in a very intentional way, the human condition." We observe other presidents echoing this appeal as they attempt to stimulate in their institutions this kind of connectedness to the real world. The imperative for institutional outreach is felt more fervently by top university leadership than by others in the academic community.

Of immediate relevance is the discussion taking place among presidents and chancellors about the role of libraries in the high-tech information age. They see a natural community of interest between libraries and academic computer centers because both deal in "information." We have already seen, for example, that Levine believes the traditional college campus will soon be replaced by computer networks. Langenberg (1993) has declared that the university library has become "obsolescent" (Langenberg, 1993). Administrative reorganization has brought libraries and computer centers together to take better advantage of this commonality of interest.

Thus, presidents and chancellors have a stake in seeing that their institutions are at the cutting edge of modern-day technology, reflecting the best thinking nationally in this regard. In addition, the economic context within which the institution must operate requires cost-effective decision making. Merging library and academic computer center resources is a tantalizing way to kill two birds with one stone—it enhances the use of technology while also promoting cost effectiveness.

*Other Academic Administrative Leaders.* Central figures in campus debates over the role of libraries in the technological age are the academic "middle managers," principally the deans and the key directors. Deans of the line academic colleges, while often included in central campus planning activities, are seen as legitimate advocates of the interests of their colleges. They see other colleges and academic support services as competitors for scarce resources. Although college deans may recognize the importance of libraries and computer centers for addressing the needs of their faculty and students, they nonetheless prefer that cuts—if cuts need to be made—be levied against the support services rather than against the teaching and research activities.

Library and academic computer center directors are in a difficult political position because of this. University librarians often carry administrative rank comparable to that of a dean. They must adopt a campus perspective that responds to the needs of the faculty and students and must compete for resources with the deans of traditional colleges. Even though the traditional deans clearly see themselves as competing with other deans for scarce resources, they have a greater sense of identity with these colleagues who have an identifiable faculty and student body and face problems similar to their own. The university librarian is in a more ambiguous position, having less well-defined faculty and student constituencies and carrying broad service responsibilities. Thus the university librarian becomes more dependent than the line college deans on the good will and support of the campus president and provost.

*Academic Support Managers.* A significant conceptual problem with important political ramifications is how university librarians should be classified. Are they campus academic leaders or managers of an academic support enterprise? This ambiguity lies at the heart of the politics of the issues at hand. The way in which it is resolved will determine the course for the development of university libraries in the years ahead.

There are managerial roles that are clearly not frontline academic leadership roles. Included among these are directors of student affairs operations (admissions and records officers, student counseling personnel, financial aid directors, and so on), research support managers, and academic human resource directors. Other clearly nonacademic officers play important roles supportive of the academic enterprise. The business officers, the physical plant operatives, campus security directors, and nonacademic personnel managers are examples. Key managers on the "other side of the house," as discussed earlier, tend to be closely aligned with the chancellor or president and can constitute an important power resource for campus leadership. They may, however, bring their influence to bear in presidential decision making on a wide variety of issues, academic as well as nonacademic, through the exercise of personal persuasion. Given the economic factors already noted, the university business officer is in an increasingly critical position for the exercise of personal influence on a number of fronts.

Conceptually, it would be appropriate to place the university librarian in this category. The library has a clear mission to support the university's core teaching and research functions. However, there are other issues involved. How do other key actors view the head librarian? How does the university librarian view his or her own role in this regard? Does the role really involve academic leadership functions or is it limited to support functions? The larger question is a normative one: What kind of role should these managers play in the development of informational resources and policies on university campuses of the twenty-first century? This issue will be given further attention as we sketch out a desirable scenario for future developments.

*Faculty.* Deep down, most faculty members believe the university revolves around their interests. It is the role of the faculty in the governance and in the performance of the institution, the concept of the collegium already discussed, that sets universities apart from other organizations. Faculty members are more than workers, they are managers as well, and this notion has some legal standing. A key issue here has to do with the boundaries of the collegium. The distinction between "locals" and "cosmopolitans" has been used to characterize university faculties for some time. The locals, preoccupied with issues involving their own campus, devote considerable time and effort to instruments of governance such as faculty senates and college and department faculty bodies. For many faculty members, however, especially at a research university, the campus is not the principal point of identification. These cosmopolitans are preoccupied with matters of their own discipline and research interests and identify more closely with colleagues at other universities, nationally and even internationally.

The development and expansion of E-mail and the Internet have facilitated enormously the ability of research faculty members to communicate continuously and effortlessly with colleagues around the world. The communication does not require being in one's office or laboratory at the university. This kind of faculty member's attitude toward the university can be quite pragmatic. Are the requisite facilities, including library, available to help them do their work wherever they may chose to do it? Is there the appropriate state of the art electronic technology allowing them to conduct business with their students?

The electronic revolution has profoundly changed the face of the university and the ways in which faculty members conduct their business, both instruction and research. It also profoundly affects the politics of institutional development and the role of the university librarian. This matter will be considered shortly.

*Students.* Internally, students make up by far the largest constituency. From the students' perspective, the university exists to serve their interests. This perspective is shared by much of the public and particularly by the parents who are footing the bills. Much of the support services addresses the needs of the students. So there is a potential common political bond between the support services and the student body. For the faculty, there is also a potential political bond with the students, but for many faculty members this bond is only rhetorical.

The student body does not constitute a strong independent political force. Students tend not to have the requisite organization for political effectiveness. In addition, the kind of centrifugal force the electronic revolution is exerting on other elements of the university is affecting the students' use of the campus as well. They too can do much of their work from remote sites. They can access the library and utilize the university's mainframe computer from a PC at home; they can interact with professors and submit papers and exams electronically.

I do not mean to say that the student body has no political relevance and will not be an important player in the development of the university of the next century. Especially if effectively joined with the faculty, students can become an important element of this process.

## Politics for Developing the University of the Twenty-First Century

The discussion in this chapter began with three primary assumptions: (1) the university of the twenty-first century will be fundamentally different from the one that we have known; (2) this change will occur within a context of limited resources; and (3) this change will occur through the operation of a political process. The first assumption is rather unexceptional given the degree to which the university has already changed. The second seems warranted by contemporary events, written as this is at the outset of the "Gingrich Revolution" and the Republicans' Contract With America and its emphasis on balanced budgets, pared-down government, and increased individual responsibility. The kinds of institutional change this volume discusses is not likely to come, in the short term, from massive infusions of money from any source.

Thus, developing an effective and responsive internal political process becomes all the more imperative. With an overarching goal of developing a university that maximizes the benefits of state of the art information technology, what is the nature of an appropriate internal political process? This question can be dealt with from the perspectives of the key stakeholders.

**University Administrative Leadership.** Presidents and chancellors may not be able to lead their institutions to the promised land merely through their vision and prescience. Indeed, to think they can may be a terrible strategic error. However, they can set the tone for a serious universitywide consideration of their institution's future and the future of all higher education. All campus constituencies must be made to understand that significant change is in the offing and that it is in their vital interest to take an active stance in the process that will lead to a changed institution. Presidents and chancellors must also point out the wisdom of paying attention to public interests rather than focusing on internal affairs in an attempt to preserve the university of the past. There are important players outside the confines of the university and the academic world in general.

The chancellor's message to the university community has to be straightforward: change will come and it will have to be accomplished with the present level of resources, at best. The immediacy and gravity of the situation can be conveyed by convening a broad-based long-range planning exercise in which the various parameters of the plan are articulated and a list of specific outcomes drawn up. Representatives of the various stakeholders should be invited to consider carefully their interests within this context. Participants should be instructed to identify the core interests of the university as a collective enterprise—what should be retained from the past as the university attempts to meet the challenges of the future. Presidents and chancellors must also exert influence on other administrative officers, in particular the deans, to engage in this process with a straightforward and universitywide approach. The current fascination with an "every tub on its own bottom" approach, which pits college against college, is short term in its effects and militates against the development of an integrated total university perspective. Finally, campus administrative leadership must be prepared to take a continuing and active role in the deliberations and support the recommendations that emerge from the process by providing for their implementation.

**The Library.** It is shortsighted to declare the university library obsolescent, even though it must change its role and mode of operation. The library must assume a leadership position in helping define and implement a vision of the university for the twenty-first century. Many of the library's traditional functions need not and should not be abandoned. Many in the faculty and student body will continue to depend on its traditional services. However, the university library cannot stand idly by and allow others to define its new role and prescribe its functions. To prevent this, it must do all it can to solidify its political position on campus so that it can play a major role in the planning process. The library must be recognized as a core element of the academic enterprise rather than peripheral to it, a focal point for the development of an advanced information-based university for the next century. Seeing the library solely as an academic support makes it easy to give its function a secondary status, thus making it vulnerable to the budgetary knife. Enlightened campus leadership might prevent this, but such an important issue should not be left to chance.

Strengthening the political capacity of the library is not a simple matter. It requires constant attention. Following are some imperatives for action:

*A strengthened academic role for the university librarian.* The university librarian must carry an administrative rank equivalent to a college dean and be prepared to play a central role in the council of deans, a key campus academic planning committee. This is the case whether a separate library school exists or not. In fact, the university librarian is in a more advantageous position to exercise campus leadership in information technology development than is the dean of an inevitably small, separate library school. Although the university librarian may be particularly well equipped for leadership in the specialized area of information technology, he or she must be also prepared to make contributions in the general area of academic program development. The librarian's credibility can be strengthened if he or she possesses a Ph.D. degree and is active in national professional circles. In addition to being expert in various dimensions of advanced information technology, it would be useful to hold academic rank in a substantive academic field. All this suggests broadened criteria for the selection of university librarians and their earlier training.

*Faculty rank for librarians.* Key library personnel should carry faculty rank and be expected to carry on scholarly activities. Their promotion in academic rank should come through regular faculty promotion and tenure processes rather than through a separate administrative process. Again, this should be the case whether the campus has a separate library school or not. The library faculty members should be full and active participants in campus faculty governance activities such as the senate and various important academic committees.

*Collaboration between librarians and faculty members.* Library faculty members should work closely with colleagues in other academic disciplines, demonstrating their usefulness in addressing various information technological needs. This requires that library personnel remain current on state of the art information technology, that the library be viewed as the place to come for help in this regard. Students should also be able to see libraries in this way rather than merely as places that warehouse books and are good to study in. Joint research projects with colleagues across campus would be an effective means for integrating the library faculty into the larger academic community.

*Curriculum development.* The library should consider developing curricula, credit or noncredit, that would be available to students and faculty alike. Noncredit workshops and short courses could be offered on a continuing basis to deal with various aspects of information technology. Credit course packages could be designed in collaboration with regular undergraduate or graduate programs to help integrate information technology into academic programming.

*Short-term appointments.* The appointment of faculty members from various campus disciplines to revolving short-term positions in the library should be considered. These positions, awarded on a competitive basis, would encourage collaborative research efforts involving library and nonlibrary faculty members in the development of substantive information technologies.

*Changed priorities in training.* New directions for the training of university library personnel are clearly implied. However, the changes involve new emphases rather than a wholesale change in professional orientation. The effective librarian of the future must be the professional who links the teacher and researcher to state of the art information technologies.

All of these notions have merit. In the main, they suggest a more proactive stance on the part of the library as the university prepares for the twenty-first century. Good policy makes good politics as well. High-profile activities that link the library closely with important faculty and student constituencies enhance the political base of the library and ultimately its possibilities for influencing the course of university development. This approach would be a significant means for changing the library's identity as an academic support mechanism to one of a central player.

**Faculty and Students.** Rather than remain blind defenders of the past who are committed to creating duplicates of themselves as they train their graduate students, faculty members should take the lead in reexamining their disciplines, where they should be going, and how they can more effectively utilize the benefits of emerging information technology. This is not to say that the traditions and history of the disciplines are irrelevant. However, a self-conscious examination of the core values of the disciplines that must be retained as the academy moves toward a fundamentally new stage of development is called for.

This reevaluation should not be done for the students but with the students. Students should be invited and encouraged to participate in a planning process that will have significant impact on their developing careers. Furthermore, student participation should not be confined to the graduate student body; undergraduates should be involved as well. In fact, there should be a fundamental shift in the way students are regarded by the mature academic community. Rather than consumers of what the university has to offer, students at all levels should be seen as active participants in the production of knowledge, in many respects junior colleagues who have something to offer in the search for knowledge. Such an attitude makes a good deal of sense in this age of rapidly developing information technology. The young have grown up in this context and are more adept and comfortable with it than many faculty members. It also makes a good deal of political sense. Reinforcing the notion that faculty and students are involved in an important common enterprise will contribute to the development of a vital force to advance core academic interests.

## A Creative Response to the External Environment

The university of the twenty-first century cannot afford to retreat behind ivy-covered walls. Instead, it must demonstrate to significant interests in the larger community its usefulness and importance. In this revolutionary age of information technology development, it can provide ideas and direction so that the technology does not outrun society's ability to use it profitably. The university is also in an advantageous position to reach out with important informational resources to diverse elements in society. This can be done in a variety of ways, from offering extension courses and programs, to providing access to the Internet and other networks to community groups, to working with elementary and secondary school systems to ensure that they benefit from the technological revolution. Such activities are good policy and very good politics. To mount effective initiatives will, however, necessitate a reordering of institutional priorities and some change in practice. Such a reordering will ultimately depend on the workings of the internal political process, a process in which the university library can and must play a significant leadership role.

## References

Baldridge, J. V., Curtis, D. V., Ecker, G. R., and Riley, G. L. "Alternative Models of Governance in Higher Education." In G. L. Riley and J. V. Baldridge (eds.), *Governing Academic Organizations: New Problems, New Perspectives.* Berkeley, Calif.: McCutchan, 1977.

Boyer, E. L. "Creating the New American College." *Chronicle of Higher Education,* Mar. 9, 1994, p. A48.

"In 2050, Computer May Be Collegian's 'Campus.'" *Chicago Tribune,* Nov. 7, 1994, p. 5.

Langenberg, D. N. "(R)evolution in American Higher Education." *UIC News,* Jan. 20, 1993, p. 11.

Sykes, C. J. *PROFSCAM: Professors and the Demise of Higher Education.* New York: St. Martin's Press, 1990.

*RICHARD M. JOHNSON is professor of political science and former vice-chancellor for academic affairs at the University of Illinois at Chicago.*

*Advances in information technology are only the latest transformation
of the printed word. Review of the research habits of humanists
suggests that print libraries will continue to be used by scholars for
some time.*

# The Disappearance of the Library: Issues in the Adoption of Information Technology by Humanists

*William Goodrich Jones*

Recent forecasts about the future of our society include two significant elements: (1) there will be great reliance on market economies to shape social, political, and technological change, and (2) the "information revolution" will extend to every sector of American society ("To Dance with Change," 1994). Higher education will be transformed by vocationalism, technological competition, and privatization of services. In the future, universities will have to compete more effectively in the marketplace for students, will become smaller and more efficient in teaching, and will employ technologies of all kinds to achieve these ends.

These are revolutionary pronouncements for institutions that have often been insulated from the demands of the marketplace and that grant faculty members six years to prove their competence (indeed, many more than six years may pass before faculty contribute substantially to a corpus of research), reward them with lifetime employment, and provide them with sabbaticals and research leaves to concentrate fully on scholarship.

In the humanities, scholars usually accord libraries high prestige. The metaphor of the library as laboratory of the humanist is one justification for investing in its resources. Consequently, it is of particular interest and a matter for informed discussion that some university administrators forecast that libraries will eventually be replaced by electronic information sources. Among these, Donald N. Langenberg, chancellor of the University of Maryland, has declared that the "library as we know it is obsolescent" (Langenberg, 1993a). Langenberg suggests that the greatest challenge for campus administrators in

the future will be to decide what to do with their library buildings (Langenberg, 1993b).

Forecasts of a paperless society have been popular for some time. The
tremendous growth in the market for personal computers and the opportunities for linking users and computerized data bases through telecommunications systems have encouraged futurists seriously to consider how such
possibilities might be realized. Former New York Public Library president Var-
tan Gregorian has suggested that an on-line reference library of 10,000 volumes be made available to every high school in the country (Stecklow, 1994).
The Library of Congress recently announced a project to digitize significant
parts of its research collection for access by scholars (Sheppard, 1994), the Bibliothèque Nationale (Paris, France) hopes to have 150,000 to 200,000 volumes
available in electronic format in 1995 (Jamet and Waysbord, 1993), and dic-
tionaries and encyclopedias are now frequently included in the preloaded software accompanying new personal computers. The number of bibliographic
and full-text data bases that are accessible through the Internet is growing daily
(Coates, 1994).

## Nature of Research in the Humanities

Scholars in the humanities are among the principal users of library collections.
Understanding how humanists have adapted to the introduction of information technologies in libraries may offer insights to campus administrators who
are shaping the evolution of campus support services. A longitudinal study of
humanists conducted since 1987 at the University of Illinois at Chicago, by
William Goodrich Jones and Stephen E. Wiberley, Jr., confirms that research
in the humanities is lonely, almost monastic, and sometimes dangerous (Wiberley and Jones, 1989, 1994). Humanists are essentially solitary workers, accustomed to spending hours with textual materials, whatever the format, and
required to do so by the methodologies of the humanities. Close reading of
texts and a mastery of the contents of a large number of documents are neces-
sities. The availability of sophisticated computer technologies has not yet
changed these habits of scholarship although the technologies have changed
the ways in which most scholars create the product of their research, the scholarly monograph. But humanists still inspect books and manuscripts in their
original form and speak of the excitement and sense of discovery that accompanies the handling of them, sometimes in remote and even politically turbulent locations in which their safety is at risk.

Important collections are often located in the geographical regions where
their contents originated. Great research centers like the Huntington Library
in Pasadena, California, the University of Chicago's Regenstein Library, or the
Newberry Library in Chicago have collections of such richness that they sometimes serve as acceptable alternatives to travel to exotic locations, even if they
do not altogether eliminate the need for it. In other cases, there is no substitute, whether the travel is to sites like Grand Forks, North Dakota, where the

personal papers of a local congressperson are held or to a small college library in the Pacific Northwest that houses a collection of master's theses on voting patterns in regional third-party political movements.

Having rare research materials in digitized formats promises to be a boon to humanistic scholarship but scholars have had such materials available already, sometimes through interlibrary loan, photographic reproduction, or microform. The principal benefit to the scholar will be the speed with which such sources become available, not the fact that they are available. Availability has always been possible for those with the means to pay for some form of reproduction or for travel to the archives that hold the material.

Although there is great optimism about the feasibility of converting to electronic form substantial portions of the print record, particularly the secondary literature, the bulk of the manuscript record cannot reasonably be digitized in the foreseeable future. The economics of doing so systematically prohibits the transformation of materials in anything but moderate or high demand. Countless repositories throughout the world contain masses of manuscript materials from the Middle Ages to the present that have not been looked at since the time of their creation; a wealth of documents of research interest also still resides in private hands. Undeniably, once a research resource becomes available electronically it may be made available to anyone with the necessary electronic equipment anywhere in the world; however, we are a long way from agreeing on how archival materials might be identified and accessed through network connections. We must also resolve a host of legal issues relating to ownership, fair use, rights and permissions, and mechanisms for payment of royalties.

## Electronic Mail

In time humanists may find it more convenient than it is now to correspond with colleagues through electronic mail. Today electronic mail is an attractive medium for those who work collaboratively, not for the solitary humanist. Humanists interviewed by Wiberley and Jones (1989) report that they reveal relatively little about their research to others. Their reasons range from difficulty in finding sympathetic and knowledgeable readers to concern that others may use material from their documentary sources that they would prefer to describe for the first time themselves.

The reliance of humanists on original source materials in locations that offer collections of depth and breadth suggests that there will never be a time when they can forgo travel to conduct their work. Furthermore, scholars are distinguished by their specializations. One of the incentives for pursuing a particular line of specialization is the opportunity it provides for travel to unusual and interesting locales and for meeting knowledgeable and colorful personalities. Scholars have been aided (and sometimes impeded) in their search for sources by local history buffs, booksellers, parish priests, mayors, and owners of privately held collections, as well as by the staffs of libraries and archives.

## Uses of Information Technology in the Sciences

Sociologists John Walsh and Todd Bayma have studied how scientists in universities use computers to communicate with each other, or as they describe it, utilize "computer mediated communication" or CMC (Walsh and Bayma, in press). Walsh and Bayma argue that work groups adopt technology that fits their organization and environment. In the case of experimental biologists, chemists, mathematicians, and physicists, the existing disciplinary structure was not much altered by the introduction of computer communication although several of those groups now use CMC heavily. One of the predictors of E-mail use is whether social groups are loosely or tightly "coupled." Biologists, for example, work in self-contained laboratories that conduct local experiments. They have less need for rapid communication with those outside their laboratories and have not adopted a standard word processor as mathematicians have. Perhaps because biologists use more pictures in their work they rely more heavily on fax than on E-mail.

Both mathematicians and physicists have solved the problem of representing their special symbolic language for electronic communication and have adopted TeX, a software system used for typesetting text, especially mathematical text. Although mathematicians are described as a solitary people who largely work alone, they have a tradition of face-to-face communication through encounters at conferences. Mathematicians now appear to use those contacts to identify collaborators with whom they might continue joint projects, and E-mail has probably contributed significantly to an increase in jointly authored papers in mathematics. For example, international collaboration leading to publication among mathematicians increased from 8.8 percent in 1986 to 17.1 percent in 1991.

Physicists use expensive one-of-a-kind machines to conduct their experiments. They work in large, dispersed teams where rapid communication with all team members is important. Chemists, working within a tradition that emphasizes a close relationship between laboratory and marketplace, are more likely to use CMC for data base searching of such sources as *Chemical Abstracts* and to rely on standard forms of publication to disseminate the results of their work. The impact of CMC on physics is that it has reduced the marginalization of physicists not located at research centers where experiments are conducted. There are now opportunities for physicists from institutions of all sizes to participate in experiments during the summer and then return to their own laboratories to conduct further analyses. The ability to communicate with their colleagues through E-mail integrates them into their disciplines in ways that they could not have before E-mail's widespread adoption.

The conclusion, then, is that the organization of scientific work has not been changed as a result of computer-mediated communication but that communication has been facilitated in disciplines that already had a tradition of collaborative research. There has not been the same transformation in the humanities primarily because of the nature of humanistic inquiry. In addition, humanists are not supplied as abundantly with computer technology as scientists are.

## The Library, the Administrator, and the Humanist

All scholarly activity requires a large investment of time. Information technology has greatly improved the ability of scholars to create documents and share them with others who are interested. Although much fanfare accompanies announcements about the public availability of documents and data on the Internet, it is the ability to use information technology to create new documents and to share them in prepublication forms with other scholars that has been of greatest use to academics.

Others have also noted that it is in the sciences that opportunities for electronic communication have been most vigorously utilized (Stix, 1994). The solitary humanist has relatively little need to communicate research results rapidly. Face-to-face communication at conferences meets many needs. However, even that is not indispensable.

There is widespread conviction among administrators that information technologies in the form of computers linking students and faculty will increasingly be required for instruction. It is assumed that all scholars will eventually acquire them. It is then only a short step to the realization of the virtual campus, an entity that need not exist in any one geographic location.

If by some means most of the secondary literature consulted by humanists were to be available only in electronic form then of course humanists would make use of it in that form just as sources available only in microfiche or microfilm are used by them now. Humanists don't much like to use microform technology but they do so because they have no other choice. They indicate, however, that the habits of conducting scholarly work are complex and time consuming and not reducible to formulaic patterns. In a world of electronic texts humanists will surely create paper copies from the electronic record and make annotations on them, just as they now do with photocopies, and they will annotate, file, and organize these paper formats much as they do now. The demand by humanists for more sophisticated hardware and university-supported network connections will expand regardless of the frequency with which humanists employ it, and this use will continue alongside the use of paper, microform, and photographs. At the same time, university administrators will be required to act as if information technology were as beneficial as its promoters claim, even if the reality fails to match the expectation. The university will pay for this equipment, either through direct subvention or through faculty salaries. Humanists have been accustomed to supporting their own research for some time. They pay for much of their travel, and they buy their own computers. They keep their computers for a long time and when they buy new ones they find other uses for the old machines. Administrators have little incentive to modify this kind of funding pattern although they may try to encourage greater reliance on telecommunications systems for use in teaching by increasing the number and accessibility of network connections.

Administrators view the library's need for resources as unending. It will require considerable restraint for those who allocate support service budgets not to suppose that the library's print collections, and particularly its quickly dated journal collections, are resources that can be given up for hardware acquisition, full-text data bases, and licensing agreements. Electronic resources, although expensive, do not need to be housed in a large building that is expensive to maintain, and they do not need staffs to reshelve them, repair them when they are damaged, and replace them when they are lost or stolen. Because of the sciences' reliance on current literature and their movement toward issuing that literature in electronic form, administrators will increasingly look to the sciences for a model.

Improved monitoring of the use of electronic data sources may permit universities to move toward a more direct method of allocating costs so that departments and colleges having the heaviest information consumers may also be expected to bear a greater portion of providing financial support for their maintenance. Science and engineering departments, long a rich source of indirect cost revenue, have always argued that they should receive a share of library support that matches their contribution. Because these departments often have their own sources of income, they are likely to become "information-rich" as others scramble to secure what limited resources remain. This would be a very different model from the present, where the campus library and the computer center have allocated their resources to support the entire community. Such a shift in policy would reflect the new interest in applying market considerations in the academy in the same way they are being applied to social policy.

## Library as Place

Langenberg's prediction that administrators will face the dilemma of what to do with their library buildings should provoke all members of the scholarly community to consider if and when planning for this disappearance ought to begin. Langenberg conceives of a world in which words that are inscribed on surfaces like paper, parchment, or stone may be equated with their representation on a computer screen. If one were to accept Langenberg's viewpoint, the issue then would become one of deciding what, if anything, should be preserved in physical form and what should be dispensed with. With the exception of the spoken word, few words today do not begin on computer screens even if they are intended sooner or later for imprinting on the page. We might assume that any words that have originated electronically are being preserved electronically, but we have no evidence to assure us that is the case. It is important therefore that standards for the preservation of electronic text be developed as soon as possible (Lynch, 1994).

The justification for converting words that now exist only in print or manuscript to electronic format is that it will bring them cheaply and quickly to audiences who are unable to inspect the originals. Furthermore, availability will presumably accompany changes in instruction from teaching-centered and on-site to learning-centered and remote. Because of the availability of electronic texts to almost anyone, the means by which ideas become available in society will be greatly democratized. It is an article of faith that electronic images will have lifetimes far exceeding their material counterparts, that the costs of distributing these images will be supportable, that everyone who desires access will have it, and that the importance of distinguishing between original and copy will be minimized or eliminated.

## Historical Models

Ours is not the first age of transformation of the written word. The transformations brought about by the invention of the printing press are well known; the invention of the steam press introduced others. But a transformation of another kind has been under way for some years. Large numbers of valuable resources have been and are being converted from paper to microform, and in these projects original sources are often destroyed. In many instances, the originals are on the point of disintegration and the loss of the originals is both unmourned and unpreventable. Projects of this kind are presently the principal measures of ensuring that texts printed on acid-laden paper in danger of disintegration are preserved, although forms of preservation through scanning and digitization are being explored. Although much has been accomplished, the achievements to date are not sufficient. Microform sources offer many advantages: they are durable, compact, and relatively inexpensive. As recently as 1990 one library director argued that the entire corpus of secondary literature ought to be converted to microform (Smith, 1990).

We have noted that humanists don't like reading microform; they appear not to like reading sources on a computer screen any better. In addition, the technology for printing paper copies from the microform has never been good. In contrast, the technology of printing from electronic sources is already well advanced and will continue to improve.

There are now scholarly sources that only exist in microform (or even microprint). Planning for the disappearance of the library must include the conversion of important microform sources to electronic format. The wealth of experience of those who have overseen those preservation projects can be applied to this new phase of image transformation. However, large numbers of original documents are far too valuable to permit destruction following conversion to electronic form. They have such strong association value or are aesthetically so important that they must be preserved in physical form, regardless of electronic accessibility. Most academic libraries have some collections that fall into this category but many will not be able to justify the expense of housing them and will be required either to sell them, give them away, or warehouse them, leaving them untended and unaccessible to a scholarly community.

## Courses of Action

The variety of formats in which research libraries preserve their documentary sources will require the continued presence of libraries for some time. But it is also likely that the competition between electronic and print sources will lead to more densely occupied libraries, to print collections that grow at a more controlled rate, and to smaller staffs to service these collections. Money for new construction, for additions, or for storage annexes will not be plentiful and will only be gained after hard competition with other worthwhile programs, some of them focusing on the electronic literature. Pressure for creating regional consortia and computerized acquisition may make collaborative collections development a reality so that fewer titles in print format need be acquired by each institution. The restructuring of higher education by boards of higher education may lead to rounds of mergers and acquisitions with the same results that have been obtained in the corporate world.

These developments will encourage some administrators to downsize smaller academic libraries, their branches, or subject collections, transforming them into electronic text centers. Such centers, supplementing the resources available to faculty and students through their own computers, might contain terminals, high-speed printers, wideband transmission capabilities that offer rapid access to electronic text archives, and telephone and videophone connections to service staff, none of which need be located in one place. Photocopy and scanning equipment might be provided to facilitate reproduction of text from those print collections that remain.

Administrators cannot prevent these developments. But it is not likely that there will be either resolve or resources to pay for the grand conversion of the existing print record, much less the manuscript record, to an electronic format, whether through scanning or digitization, even if current scholarly publishing becomes almost entirely electronic. A political climate that emphasizes prioritizing social issues according to market principles and that grapples with demands for health care, elementary and secondary education, social security, welfare, the common defense, and prison construction is not likely to devote much attention to problems surrounding the preservation of the scholarly record. Such a climate may diminish the importance of that record, and neglect and even malice may lead to dispersal and destruction with irreversible consequences.

## Conclusion

Donald Langenberg's dismissal of libraries as "obsolescent" is surely premature, although the confidence of administrators in print libraries as symbols of culture and academic learning has declined. The world of print is hard pressed to compete with the promotional campaigns of an industry that receives $160 billion annually in spending by business for computers and related services. Electronic publishing, however, is still in its infancy and is beset by problems associated with high costs and an uncertain market. Information technology has transformed the conduct of inquiry in the sciences, making a great impact on the means by which scientists communicate with one other, but it has yet to make such a transformation in the humanities.

The library building is not likely to disappear. However, its survival as a quiet place for reading and reflection will be greatly affected by changing attitudes about what educated people need to know, the way in which they need to know it, and the acceptance or rejection of information technology as a means of becoming educated. Humanists have been important users of library collections, and many libraries have been constructed to meet their needs. Humanists are less influential than they once were, but they are still indispensable members of university communities. Humanistic inquiry will continue in much the same way as it has. What will be most important is that humanists have access to as much of the record of print and archival sources as can be identified and preserved, be it in libraries or their offices or homes, in physical or electronic form.

## References

Coates, J. "Where the Buffalo—and the Computers—Roam." *Chicago Tribune,* Oct. 2, 1994, sec. 7, p. 5.

Jamet, D., and Waysbord, H. "History, Philosophy, and Ambitions of the Bibliothèque de France." *Representations,* Spring 1993, *42,* 74–79.

Langenberg, D. N. "The Lonely Scholar in a Global Information Environment." In *University of Iowa, Symposium on Scholarly Communication, 1991.* Westport, Conn.: Meckler, 1993a.

Langenberg, D. N. "(R)evolution in American Higher Education." *UIC News,* Jan. 20, 1993b, p. 11.

Lynch, C. "The Integrity of Digital Information: Mechanics and Definitional Issues." *Journal of the American Society for Information Science,* Dec. 1994, *45* (10), 737–744.

Sheppard, N., Jr. "Computers Recasting Humanities Research." *Chicago Tribune,* Oct. 13, 1994, sec. 1, p. 8.

Smith, E. *The Librarian, the School, and the Future of the Research Library.* New York: Greenwood, 1990.

Stecklow, S. "Man with Millions Is Seeking Schools Worth Spending It On." *Wall Street Journal,* July 26, 1994, pp. B-1, B-3.

Stix, G. "Trends in Scientific Communication: The Speed of Write." *Scientific American,* Nov. 1994, *271* (6), 106–111.

"To Dance with Change." *Policy Perspectives,* 1994, *5* (3), A1–A12.

Walsh, J. P., and Bayma, T. "Computer Networks and Scientific Work." *Social Studies of Science,* in press.

Wiberley, S. E., Jr., and Jones, W. G. "Patterns of Information Seeking in the Humanities." *College and Research Libraries,* Nov. 1989, *50,* 638–645.

Wiberley, S. E., Jr., and Jones, W. G. "Humanists Revisited: A Longitudinal Look at the Adoption of Information Technology." *College and Research Libraries,* Nov. 1994, *55* (6), 499–509.

*WILLIAM GOODRICH JONES is assistant university librarian and associate professor of library administration at the University of Illinois at Chicago.*

*What to keep and what to discard will remain very much an issue
in the era of the virtual library.*

# The Academic Library Collection
# in an On-Line Environment

*Ross Atkinson*

> Selection is the very keel on which our mental ship is built. And in
> this case of memory its utility is obvious. If we remembered every-
> thing, we should on most occasions be as ill off as if we remembered
> nothing.
> —William James (1890)

Academic libraries exist for only one purpose: to provide local users—scholars
and students—with access to the information they need for their education and
research. The library achieves that purpose by ensuring that needed sources of
information remain accessible and reliable (that is, authentic, unaltered) over
time, and by establishing conventionalized relationships among published
sources so that users can make decisions about which sources to consult and
interpret in which order. Collection building is one of the primary means used
by the library to ensure access and establish source relationships. Based on
assessments and assumptions of the current and future information needs of
local users, the library selects, assembles, and maintains certain publications,
and in so doing relates those publications to each other, guarantees their continued existence, boosts their access for local purposes (effectively inserting
them into local research and instruction), and privileges them with respect to
the much larger universe of publication that exists beyond the collection.

We stand now at the edge of an information revolution sparked by
advances in computer technology and telecommunications that will change
fundamentally both the concept of the collection in the academic library and
the role of the library in the academic institution. Many analyses have been

NEW DIRECTIONS FOR HIGHER EDUCATION, no. 90, Summer 1995   © Jossey-Bass Publishers

made of the probable future of academic information services in this rapidly approaching, primarily on-line environment. (Several excellent overviews of the thinking on the future of information services have appeared recently. See especially Lynch, 1993a; Rutstein, DeMiller, and Fuseler, 1993; and Draben-stott, 1994.) One expectation is that scholars—initially mainly in the sciences but eventually in other disciplines as well—will begin to exchange information with each other more routinely during the course of their work rather than mainly through formal publication. The result will be what has been labeled a "collaboratory" (see National Research Council, 1993; see also Clarke, 1994). Indeed, in some disciplines, this is already taking place. In a sense, therefore, the history of scholarly communication has come full circle: while the scholarly journal originated in the seventeenth century as a means to replace or broaden correspondence (Houghton, 1975, pp. 11–19), today a form of correspondence on the network is beginning to supplant some functions of publication. As this kind of scholarly communication increases, there are vital "knowledge management" roles that the academic library must be prepared to assume (Lucier, 1990, 1992). At the same time, however, we must not imagine, as some have, that formal publication based on peer review will become obsolete once all scholars are connected on-line. For a number of reasons, some of which will be discussed in this chapter, formal publication will remain an essential element of scholarly communication. But what happens, then, to the library collection as increasing quantities of information, both informal collaborative correspondence and formal publication, become available on-line? How should formally published information be assembled, maintained, and controlled? Can we even speak of a "collection" under such circumstances? And what will become of the paper materials wedged onto the shelves of today's libraries? This chapter will consider these questions. In so doing, I hope to assist academic administrators to identify and prepare for the kinds of decisions that will need to be made to accommodate and take advantage of the new information environment.

## Three Stipulations

As we begin our discussion, we need to keep three issues in mind: the economics of attention, the educational dilemma, and the reification trap.

**The Economics of Attention.**   Richard Lanham in his recent book *The Electronic Word* (1993) has presented a number of original and relevant observations about the future of information and literacy in an increasingly on-line environment. Of the many ideas Lanham puts forward, we note especially his highly germane opinion that the scarcest resource in the information age will be the reader's attention. Because economics is the management of scarce resources, a primary challenge to educators in future will be to devise an economics of attention (pp. 225–257). The modern library in its current mostly paper condition has, of course, always faced that challenge. The purpose of the collection is precisely to permit the user to focus attention on what is relevant amidst the din of the other sources that distract the user's attention, to increase the signal-to-noise ratio. But Lanham is doubtless correct in asserting that the need for such an economics of attention will increase as we move further into an on-line environment.

**The Educational Dilemma.** Thus the library aims to keep the user focused on a particular path, to arrange and relate sources so that time is not wasted and irrelevant "noise" does not distract. At the same time, however, the current culture and philosophy of information services demand that the library leave to the user as much discretion as possible in determining what information to use and in selecting the path most fruitful to his or her research. Thus the library's perpetual and existential dilemma is to control but not to regulate information, to guide but not to lead the library user. This dilemma is faced no doubt in many forms by all educators but it is especially acute for the library. The library's expertise is not in the information it provides but rather in the provision of information; in order to make specific information accessible, however, the library is obliged to make some value judgments about it.

**The Reification Trap.** The third point that we need to bear in mind is that reality is fundamentally and unavoidably social. In contrast, publications are things. Although the function of the library is to relate these things to each other and to put people in a position to locate and understand these things, the more elemental forces that drive the library and its use are the relationships among the people using the sources rather than the relationships among the sources themselves. To imagine otherwise is to fall victim to reification. In our zeal to analyze and postulate how the library provides and manages information, therefore, we need always to bear in mind that most of what we do has its primary motivation and purpose in human relationships.

## The Traditional Academic Library Collection

To consider where we are going we must first understand where we are. Let us examine some of the concepts that underlie academic library collection building in today's paper environment.

**Three Screens.** Library collections are created primarily for economic reasons, for to provide the user with relatively immediate access to all information is neither possible nor desirable. The point of building a collection is to differentiate works added from works excluded. Even the largest research libraries acquire only a small percentage of what is actually published. Collection development is, therefore, a screening operation. Collection development functions as the central or secondary screening process in a trio of screening processes, the succession of which determines or at least significantly affects what users have access to and thus what they know from published scholarly information over time. The primary screening process today is publishing; the tertiary one is collection retention. Each of the three successive processes is intended to reduce for economic reasons (both financial and attentive) the number of publications available to the user. More is written than can or should be published, more is published than can or should be collected by libraries, more is collected than can or should be retained by libraries over time.

**Source Types and Attributes.** Although library collections are used differently by students and scholars working in different disciplines, academic library use can be divided into two broad fundamental categories, each with a corresponding source type. These are data and notification. (Certainly more source types and functions can be defined than these two. For a fuller discussion, see Atkinson, 1989, pp. 507–508, 514–515.)

*Data sources* provide or record information that is used for research purposes. They can be historical, statistical, or bibliographical. Some data sources are used to aid research (for example, reference sources) whereas others are the object of research (such as literary or historical documents). The former are used in all subjects whereas the latter, which constitute a large portion of the holdings of research libraries, are used primarily by the humanities.

*Notification sources* are publications produced by contemporary scholars for purposes of communicating with one another: these are the scholarly books and articles that often make up the bulk of our acquisitions and absorb most of our acquisitions budgets. Notification sources are the material stuff of scholarship. The faculty users of academic libraries are at once the primary consumers and producers of notification sources.

Publications are selected for most academic library collections by the library staff (usually called bibliographers or selectors). Generally speaking, the selector makes decisions based on particular attributes of available sources that, in his or her judgment, will meet the defined or assumed needs of the current, local constituency. Although the selector can identify materials that will be useful to local students or scholars and can often determine that one source will be more useful than another, there is normally no way for the selector to determine whether a work will be totally useless. In a research library almost any source can have some use; this is the universal utility syndrome.

Source attributes can be divided into two fundamental categories. Let us call them extrinsic and intrinsic. Extrinsic source attributes can be easily, or at least relatively objectively, determined. They include such features as subject, publisher, format, language, and possibly such qualities as the reputation of the author and the level of difficulty or sophistication of the work. These attributes are used not only for selection but also for cataloging and reference purposes. But the library does not and cannot fulfill its responsibilities by restricting its attention to extrinsic attributes. To fulfill its educational mission, the library must also—again, for economic reasons—try to identify intrinsic attributes, that is, the potential value or significance of the work for local users. This is a far more difficult and subjective operation, but collection building (not to mention reference services) always requires some knowledge and application of intrinsic attributes by library staff.

In the course of identifying or defining intrinsic source attributes, the library most clearly faces its educational dilemma: it must contrive to focus user attention and lead users in particular directions while at the same time allowing as much flexibility as possible to decide what to read in what order. Faculty can, of course, contribute to the identification of intrinsic attributes and their participation in the building of college library collections, which are frequently based heavily upon the current curriculum, is particularly prevalent for this reason.

Why, then, do faculty not play a larger role in the selection of materials for research libraries today? To differing degrees, the faculty are regularly consulted on research library selection decisions and policy, but there are several reasons why they cannot build research library collections. First, there is the mundane problem of time. So much is being published that selection has become a full-time profession. Second, there is the problem of collection bias. Heavy faculty selection results in unbalanced collections because certain faculty members will inevitably build more actively than others. Third, such participation is not politically or economically feasible because no institution has adequate resources for all faculty to acquire all the sources they want. Therefore, to the dismay of some faculty, there must always be an objective arbiter or agent—the library selector—who decides on the basis of systematic criteria those materials that should be acquired in the best interests of the institution as a whole.

**Publishing and Collection Development.** Collection development can only be understood in relation to the screening operation that precedes it, publication. Publishing and the library effectively divide between themselves the main responsibility in the paper environment for mediating between the writer and the reader in all aspects of formal scholarly communication. Many of the budget issues that affect collection development and indeed the operation of the library in general derive from decisions made and actions taken by the publishing industry.

In most cases of scholarly publication, especially the publication of notification sources, the author does not own what he or she produces, but rather deeds ownership through copyright to the publisher in return for publication. The modern publisher as copyright holder does not, therefore, sell information but rather sells the material sources from which information may be extracted or created and the limited right to extract that information from those sources. Even after the reader extracts or learns that information, the reader does not "own" it, that knowledge is still legally owned by the publisher. (For an especially informative review of these issues, see Okerson, 1991.) The convention of transferring the ownership of scholarly information to publishers has in some cases proven highly prejudicial to scholarly communication. So many publications have come into existence and their prices are often so high that institutions cannot afford to acquire what users legitimately need. This situation is not, I hasten to add, the fault of the publishers. The problem derives at least partially from the demands of scholars for effective publishing outlets. It should also be remembered that the primary goal of the publisher is not to exchange information (that is merely a means) but rather to increase revenue and a few publishers specializing in scholarly publication have achieved that goal spectacularly. The exchange of information is the goal of the library and the academy and entrusting that responsibility—contracting out knowledge dissemination—to publishers (especially commercial ones) has been in some instances a serious error because it increases the economic barriers to scholarly communication.

What most vexes many librarians is that the scholars who produce much of the work that librarians acquire are often at the same institutions as the librarians. In effect, scholars are giving their work to publishers who then package it and sell it back to the librarians, sometimes at extremely high prices. (Probably the most balanced and authoritative discussion of these concerns is found in Cummings and others, 1992, pp. 83–99.) However, some of this anger and anxiety probably has its source in reification. The assumption is that the purpose of publication is information exchange. But what publishers appear to know somewhat better than librarians is that scholarly publication actually has many competing purposes, one of which is communication about the author. Notification sources tell the reader not simply what the writer knows but that the writer knows it—that the writer knows something that an editorial board of experts agrees is worth communicating to other experts, that the writer belongs to that community of experts and through such publication is playing a leadership role. Thus, publication is certification. As such it is inextricably bound into the highly stylized social and cultural fabric of the academy.

We must also recognize that scholarly journals "have a natural tendency to be hierarchical, with scholars generally in agreement on the relative rankings of the journals that publish material in their fields" (Noll and Steinmueller, 1992, pp. 33). Most scholars strive, therefore, to publish in high-ranking core journals (that is, journals that are frequently cited) that have established records of articles that have contributed significantly to what is known on a subject. It has become easier for publishers to create core journals because disciplines have become so extremely specialized. Because "faculty prefer to avoid a lengthy hierarchy of journals in a discipline, in some sense all new journals are 'essential' in that they constitute a natural home for articles of value. In a sense, all journals become at least second best in the hierarchy for a small number of scholars. Hence, libraries face not only increasing average prices owing to declining average circulation, but also intense demand to subscribe to all journals because every one is in some sense important" (Noll and Steinmueller, 1992, p. 35).

Thus what the publisher aims to provide is not simply a medium through which information can be exchanged but also a mechanism that adds status to any item it accepts for publication. That is in fact the value added by the publisher. In the closed and competitive culture of the academy, the value of such a mechanism is difficult to measure in mere dollars.

**Interinstitutional Cooperation.** As the costs of library materials have consistently outpaced the ability of libraries to purchase them, libraries have resorted increasingly to interlibrary lending. (According to Stubs, 1994, pp. 6–7, interlibrary borrowing per student increased by 60 percent in academic research libraries between 1986 and 1993. During the same period subscriptions per student decreased by 14 percent and monographs purchased per student decreased by 30 percent.) This has led to efforts at interinstitutional cooperative collection development, that is, formal agreements among institutions so that different institutions take responsibility for collecting different materials. Materials can then be shared and (so goes the concept) the collections of all institutions treated as if they were our own. Without such cooperative agreements, institutions risk canceling the same journals or avoiding the purchase of the same monographs so that eventually some materials would become inaccessible. The idea therefore has been to aim for the creation of a single, national collection owned by and located at different institutions but accessible to all scholars at all institutions.

University administrations have urged this eminently logical goal on the library community for decades but, with a few exceptions, libraries have failed to achieve it. The few real successes in cooperative collection development have been regional; probably the best known of these is the arrangement between Duke, North Carolina State, and the University of North Carolina (see Dominguez and Swindler, 1993). The reasons for the low success rate are varied but clear. To begin with, we cannot share core journals or monographs. All institutions with active faculty must hold these materials if the faculty are to do their research and students are to receive instruction. Some publishers know which journals are core and charge much more for them. Most efforts at cooperative collection development, therefore, have concentrated on peripheral materials. Because the costs of these materials are often much lower this has seldom resulted in any significant dollar savings. Moreover, as the costs of core journals have increased, our ability to purchase peripheral materials has declined, which is particularly unfortunate because just such items make for rich research collections.

What makes interinstitutional cooperative collection development from the outset most difficult, however, is the *local imperative,* that is, the unremitting political pressure to spend local funds to meet local needs. The library exists to provide access to those materials its users require. A truly cooperative program would compel the use of local funds to meet national rather than local needs. For cooperation to work effectively, in other words, a library would be obliged not only to spend its budget on some materials its local users do not need but also to do so at the expense of some materials they do need. This is not something that any academic library has the political strength to achieve, nor is it something the library really wants to do even though it may claim it does. Libraries are local service bureaus. They measure their success and derive most of their rewards from responding directly to the needs of their local clientele. Library selectors are trained to empathize and identify with faculty users in order to make decisions in the best interest of those users. Thus the selector always gives precedence to the local over the national (and to the present over the future). As a result, libraries are regularly willing to duplicate material held elsewhere, even if that means that some items will not be collected anywhere and may for that reason eventually become inaccessible.

In the past year, the Association of American Universities (AAU), in collaboration with the Association of Research Libraries, has embarked upon yet another program to coordinate the acquisition of foreign materials; the initial pilot projects will concentrate on materials from Latin America, Japan, and Germany. (See Association of American Universities, 1994, pp. 1–41.) This new initiative is based upon the same synergistic method of dividing responsibilities among institutions that has always been used for cooperative collection development and it therefore will face the same obstacles, especially the local imperative. What differentiates this effort from previous ones, however, is its strong endorsement by the presidents of the AAU institutions. Although I am not certain if all of the political implications have been understood by all of the institutions involved and although I believe that most faculty will probably view such a program initially as a significant diminution of services, the new initiative is a very promising step indeed. Only the AAU presidents acting in concert could bring about such a revolutionary alteration in the academic culture.

But even with such hopes on the horizon we must not delude ourselves. Even if institutions were to succeed in binding together in this way, such a cooperative initiative would by itself be doomed to failure because libraries do not control publication prices and we are operating in a publishing environment that is a near monopoly. If institutions use cooperative collection development and interlibrary loan to subscribe to fewer journals, publishers will simply increase prices to cover revenue loss. In the long run, therefore, interinstitutional cooperation is not the answer to the crisis in the cost of library materials.

**The Weight of History.** The tertiary selection screen in the paper environment consists of retention decisions as the library decides which materials it wishes to preserve and which to withdraw. Research libraries, however, rarely practice this operation. Regular withdrawal is something done primarily by smaller libraries, public and academic, that have limited space, clearly defined user needs, and few historical obligations. Research libraries generally prefer to add more shelves (even at the expense of user space), build extensions to library buildings, and construct large off-site storage facilities when space is no longer available on central campus. The main reason for the resistance to withdrawal is the universal utility syndrome described earlier. Because any publication has potential use for research, the retention of any publication is not only justified but expected. In a way, therefore, the very act of bringing a publication into a research library collection enhances its value to such a point that we are often unable to dispense with it.

However, withdrawal is an area in which some interinstitutional cooperation should be possible. Because candidates for withdrawal are of low use, institutions should be able to coordinate withdrawals to ensure that one or two copies of individual items are retained somewhere in the country. Once again, however, libraries have, with a few regional exceptions, never managed to achieve this. One possible reason is that it could be cheaper, or at least faster (which is another form of cheaper), to store an item in a warehouse and retrieve it as needed than to find it at another institution and borrow it through interlibrary loan. Another reason is certainly that the cost of coordination would be quite high: assigning responsibility to particular institutions for specific titles and ensuring that the institutions give exceptional treatment to those titles would be an expensive undertaking. There can be no doubt, therefore, that duplicate copies of very low-use materials are being retained by research libraries throughout the country.

## Academic Library Collection On-Line

Let us now turn our attention to the library in a primarily on-line environment.

**Vision.** When compared with our present circumstances, scholarly communication in an on-line environment would at first glance appear to be something approaching an information utopia. Because everyone in the country or in the world would in theory have access to a single "copy" of a publication in a single server, the long-pursued national collection could, at least technically, finally become a reality. Many of the political impediments to interinstitutional cooperation, and most importantly many manifestations of the local imperative, would be eliminated because the amount of time required by a local user to gain access to an item of information would be the same whether the item is at the user's institution or an institution on the other side of the country. In a totally on-line client-server environment, therefore, all institutions could divide collection responsibilities, possibly in some cases in cooperation with scholarly associations. Each institution could concentrate all of its resources on building comprehensive on-line collections in narrowly defined subject areas to which all users everywhere would have access. (For example, the American Physics Society, 1991, pp. 1113, has predicted the evolution of a single physics data base.)

There would be costs, of course, in the form of equipment, programming, and telecommunications, but as the cost of some technology (especially storage) continues to decline, total costs could conceivably not exceed what all institutions now spend on the creation of separate discrete collections. A scholar specializing in a particular discipline, moreover, would no longer require that the library at his or her institution support that expertise with research-level collections built by subject experts. Those bibliographical experts, the on-line librarians who understand how to develop and service an on-line collection in that particular discipline, could be concentrated at whatever institution assumed responsibility for the subject area. The scholar could work with that remote collection as easily as if it were stored on campus and communicate on-line with the bibliographers building the collection.

In an oversimplified nutshell, the foregoing is one vision of the on-line collection of the twenty-first century. It is a somewhat naive vision, perhaps, for there are certainly significant impediments to its realization, some of which

we will examine in this chapter. It is, however, a vision toward which scholars, university administrators, and academic librarians should nevertheless
strive, for such a system would inestimably enhance scholarship and higher
education. Its realization is technically, and probably financially, feasible. The
technology needed is already emerging and academic institutions could, as a
group, by collaborating closely and pooling their funds, create this kind of distributed scholarly information network.

**Dual-Collection Adjustment.** Many academic libraries now speak in
terms of a "format-free" collection policy, by which it is meant that the objective of the library is to collect all relevant information within the confines of
available funding without regard to format. Whether the item needed is in
paper, in microform, or on-line, therefore, is irrelevant and should not influence the selection decision.

Such a "format-free" policy serves not only informational but also political purposes. It is useful in allaying concerns that the library may be purchasing less useful on-line sources at the expense of more useful (but less glitzy)
traditional paper sources. It is safe and fashionable, therefore, for libraries to
claim utility as the paramount criterion for all selection. But things are, of
course, not nearly so straightforward. To begin with, any publication's format
must always be factored into the selection decision if for no other reason than
that different formats require different kinds of support. A bibliography on
magnetic tape may provide much better access than a paper version but there
is little point in acquiring it if the equipment and programming skills necessary to make it accessible do not exist in the local institution. Even more fundamentally, we must avoid what we might call the *format fallacy,* that is, the
misdirected assumption that utility is somehow incidental to the format. That
is never the case. Utility is always at least partially a product of format. If utility is the avowed fundamental criterion for the building of library collections
then the format must (and does) play a major role in the selection decision.
On-line sources do not, therefore, constitute simply "another" format to be
equated with the traditional formats of paper and microform. There are fundamental differences between analog and digital information that libraries must
understand and exploit. If the current fashion is to downplay those differences,
this is done for political purposes or in order more easily to insert—from a
process perspective—digital information services into a library infrastructure
designed to provide access to analog information.

For some time into the future, therefore, we must be prepared to live not
so much with a two-format collection as with two separate collections, one digital and one analog, that have very different qualities, provide very different
services, and require very different relationships between users and information. If everything continues to proceed as expected, most scholarly use will
gradually shift from the analog to the digital but the transition will doubtless
take many years and be very uneven.

In order to hasten and promote the digital library, we will probably need
to do exactly what the traditionalists fear: acquire (in the sense of provide

access to, pay for) what are some initially less useful materials in digital form at the expense of more useful materials in traditional form. We will need to build a critical mass of digital materials with which users can work, a collection that can begin to compete with the analog collection for the user's attention. Eventually, the very fact that a source is on-line will begin to render it more useful than sources in traditional formats.

**Building the Digital Library Collection.** The digital library collection will be created from two sources. The first will be those materials that are directly available to the library in digital form, either because they were originally produced in that form or because, although initially in analog form, they were converted to digital form. The second will be materials that the library owns in some analog form and then decides to convert to digital form. (For a summary of projects currently under way to convert analog information to digital form, see Drabenstott, 1994, pp. 111–122.)

Although the first category will be subject to special selection problems already described (notably the need for adequate support and infrastructure), many of the criteria now used for the selection of analog materials can be used to make decisions on publications already in on-line form. We must assume that digital versions of both data sources and notification sources will be published initially by a variety of for-profit and not-for-profit publishers as well as by some individuals who take advantage of the network to become their own publishers. Libraries may add selected sources to their collections either by loading the publications on tape, disk, or another medium into local servers, or by linking to the publications on remote servers. If managed correctly, the local user should notice no difference between the two.

Far more problematical will be the full-text retrospective conversion to digital form of a carefully selected subset of materials that the library already owns in analog form. This will require entirely new selection criteria for which we have few models in the traditional library. Another difficulty in this process will be a political manifestation of the format fallacy: if we are suffering from such severe budget pressures, some will ask, why devote our scarce and shrinking resources to making another copy of something we already own? To ask such a question is to assume that the business of the library is to acquire symbols on surfaces and that once those symbols have been received, cataloged, and stored, the library's job is done. However, the business of the library is not to acquire but rather to provide access to symbols on surfaces, to relate those sources to each other, and to relate users to those sources. Mere ownership never accomplishes that (even in the analog environment). If by converting publications to digital form we substantially enhance their accessibility and utility, then such conversion is fully justified, even if it must be done at the expense of providing access to other unowned information.

Thus conversion is an entirely new form of selection. We must also bear in mind that the use of information in analog form will necessarily decline over time. Analog information that is not converted will become increasingly obscure. It must be the library's responsibility, therefore, in building the (national) digital collection to decide which materials in analog form are to be injected into the digital collection, to compete there for the user's attention.

How exactly do we decide what to move from the analog to the digital collection? This is a difficult question that will cause considerable controversy for many years to come. Initially we will probably want to undertake some large-scale conversion projects in which certain kinds of materials for use in particular disciplines or research projects will be converted en masse. But I would also strongly urge a parallel approach. What is converted should be at least partially driven by what is being published, in the sense of what sources are cited in current on-line publications. It should become one of the routines of on-line publishing that as many of the paper publications as possible cited in an on-line notification source be converted to on-line form so that a hyper-text link between the citation and the item can be established. Admittedly, this will lead in the beginning to an odd collection of digitized materials. Some obscure items that happen to have been cited will be in digital form while some fundamentally important core materials remain in paper. Quickly, however, many of the core materials should become digitized in this way and the content of the digital library will grow based on what active scholars are actually using. Scholars will themselves define the significant publications in their fields by citing those in the notification sources they produce. (In a sense, this continues the tradition of preservation through copying that has been in effect since antiquity: the publications preserved are those that scholars and librarians at the time deem important enough to justify copying.)

**The Primary Impediment.** What stands in the way of achieving these goals? Neither technology nor lack of funding (for we do have the funding, if we are prepared to use it for these purposes) nor lack of vision nor even political opposition. All of these can be overcome through some combination of planning and will power. What truly stands in our way is ownership: even though we have paid publishers large sums of money for paper publications we do not own the information content. Even though our faculty have produced large portions of that information neither they nor their institutions own it. We cannot therefore decide to convert our analog holdings to digital form because some owners—some publishers—will not permit it or at least not without what will no doubt be prohibitive prices. (The position of the Association of American Publishers was presented in a press release [August 5, 1994]: "Reproduction is an exclusive right of the copyright holder; therefore, scanning, a form of reproduction, generally requires the permission of the copyright holder. Since the copyright law already addresses reproduction, *no new right is necessary* to deal with scanning.") We are rapidly approaching a point, therefore, at which we may finally have the technology to provide equal access for all scholars everywhere to much of what is published but will be unable to provide that access partially because we have had the poor judgment to transfer away the legal control over the information itself.

**Publishing Future Notification Sources.** Clifford Lynch has warned us not to become preoccupied with publishing, "which is on . . . [our] minds because of the pricing crisis. But publishing is only a part of (and, in some sense, a byproduct of) the overall system of scholarly communication, which is much larger and more complex" (Lynch, 1992, p. 111). This is certainly true. As noted earlier, libraries do have a major reference services role to play in assisting informal communication, which is becoming increasingly central to scholarship in some disciplines. But formal publication will remain essential to scholarly communication. Indeed, it may become even more vital in the on-line environment where so much information will be immediately accessible and reader attention will be in increasingly short supply. It will be through the formal publication process (that is, involving peer review) in on-line form that primary screening must continue to occur. The alternative would be informational chaos. Through peer review, the scholarly community will separate out core information, so that the scholar or the novice will know to concentrate his or her attention upon that information first.

If we assume that the current client-server model continues to evolve and eventually most notification sources are created and disseminated on-line as electronic publications that replace paper books and journals, how will publication of notification sources be accomplished? Let us posit two general scenarios.

The first scenario, which we will call the *commercial model,* is a replication in the on-line environment of the publisher-author-library relationship that now exists. Each publishing house will own by virtue of copyright its particular publications. Scholars will continue to sign over the ownership rights of their writings in return for publication. The publisher will mount those publications in one or more privately owned servers. Local users—scholars and students—will then access the remote server of the publisher. The institution—probably but not necessarily the library—will be billed in some way either for each publication in the server accessed by a local user (the "by-the-drink" option) or more likely (and preferably) through some kind of site license allowing any user at the institution access to any of a set of articles in a server (the "all-you-can-eat" option). In the by-the-drink option, the user will probably be prohibited by law from transmitting a copy of the publication over the network; in the all-you-can-eat version, the user will probably be prohibited from sending the publication over the network to anyone outside the institution. This scenario will be indeed "a great irony" because "while these networks promise to largely eliminate the accidents of geography as an organizing principle for interinstitutional cooperation and to usher in a new era of cooperation among geographically dispersed organizations, the shift to licensing essentially means that each library contracting with a publisher or other information provider becomes . . . [an] isolated, insular organization that cannot share its resources with any other organization on the network" (Lynch, 1993a, p. 22). Commercial publishers will use every means at their disposal to make this scenario a reality because their survival will depend upon it.

The second scenario, which we will call the *institutional model,* represents a radical departure from the situation that now exists. The servers and their contents will be owned not by the publishers but by the institutions, possibly in collaboration with scholarly associations. Each institution will be responsible for maintaining a set of servers that hold publications based perhaps on some division of subjects among institutions; all electronic publications, or at least all formally published notification sources, of each discipline, in other words, may be held in particular servers at designated institutions. All servers will be network-accessible. Each discipline will establish editorial boards. When the boards accept an item for publication, it will be added to the appropriate server, which will then be maintained indefinitely by the institution responsible for it. The copyright will be owned by the institution responsible for the server and any item in any server should be freely accessible to anyone, provided it is not for commercial purposes. Instead of spending money to buy notification sources, institutions will spend money to make collections of notification sources available. Some of the funding currently used for the purchase of books and subscriptions in the print environment would be spent instead on client-server infrastructure and telecommunications. (For two often-cited calls for variations of the institutional model, see Rogers and Hurt, 1989, and Dougherty, 1992.)

It is likely that we will see some manifestations or combinations of both scenarios for some time into the future. One scenario, however, will eventually dominate the other. Because publishers already own large quantities of scholarly information in analog formats and because some of the more adventurous publishers will likely soon begin to publish in electronic form, some version of the commercial model is at least initially inevitable. However, it does not need to become the dominant model. If institutions move decisively, they can begin gradually to shift the "action" from commercial servers to institutional servers so that eventually most of the use falls on the latter.

It is important to recognize that on-line publication does not in and of itself improve access to information. Rather it improves the control of information and such control can be used not only to enhance access but also to constrict it. If institutions do not fight to put such an open network of scholarly communication in place we will see no improvement and possibly even a degradation in access as more scholarly information becomes available on-line. Some publishers will still own the information needed by scholars and students at institutions of higher education and that information will be kept as scarce as possible in order to maintain market value.

**Three Probable Objections (of Many) to the Institutional Model.** Needless to say, the institutional model just described would be an enormous undertaking requiring the mobilization and merging of information services on each campus, in the form of the library, the computer center, the press, and possibly the bookstore, not to mention much more extensive, formal coordination among institutions than is now practiced. The extent to which the institutional model is possible will depend partially upon costs but if it is found to be within the financial reach of the academy and if we are interested in moving toward it, we need to be prepared for many concerns and objections. Three of these seem especially important.

*The complication of interinstitutional competition.* In today's environment, institutions are in constant competition with each other for the best faculty, the best students, the greatest endowment, the most grant funding. The relative availability of scholarly information at different institutions—the quality of their libraries—plays a highly visible role in this competition. Exceptional libraries attract exceptional scholars who attract, in turn, exceptional students and funding. Rich, prestigious institutions become in this way richer and more prestigious, giving poorer institutions something to which they can aspire— the American Way. So what happens to this long-established prestige relationship if all scholars, regardless of their institution, have access to the available information, or at least to most of the key, current notification sources? Bigger institutions having more funding available would presumably play a larger role in the national scholarly information effort than smaller, poorer institutions; however, the latter would have a part as well. But what advantages does the institutional model offer the larger institutions? The essential point about Harvard's library, after all, is that every institution really wants it but only Harvard has it. Harvard's library is a scarce resource. Its value depends on that very scarcity. If some of that scarcity is removed (which is what the institutional model is partially intended to accomplish over time), then some of that value is lost. Will we see a collusion, therefore, between the large commercial publishers and the great academic libraries to move toward the commercial model so that both can retain their superior positions? Probably not.

Even the great academic libraries are under severe budgetary pressures today. Even they must depend on other libraries (primarily, other research libraries) because they can no longer acquire all that they need. There is some hope, therefore, that perhaps the largest academic libraries in the country (for example, the Association of Research Libraries) could jointly identify the funds among themselves in a relatively equitable fashion to undertake something approaching the institutional model. For some time into the future, moreover, the advantages of the very wealthy academic library will remain in its analog holdings, items that will become increasingly rare because they have not been converted to digital form. It is likely, therefore, that those disciplines that rely heavily on historical materials will become more centralized at the larger institutions, which can continue to maintain large paper libraries, while those disciplines (mostly in the sciences and the professions) that depend on current notification sources will remain dispersed at institutions of all sizes.

*Loss of hierarchy.* A second problem that could block a move toward the institutional model involves the cultural function of scholarly publication discussed earlier. Some journals or publishers are seen to be more standard or "core" than others and an article or a book published through them bespeaks a greater expertise on the part of the author. If the institutional model were to be put fully into effect, many individual journals and publishers would presumably disappear (see American Physics Society, 1991, pp. 1137–38).

All scholarly publications presumably would be published in a single set of servers so that there would be little hierarchical differentiation of the kind now provided. Don Schauder (1994, pp. 93–95) uncovers a basic ideological conflict in our move toward the digital collection between the "tradition of the free sharing of academic knowledge" represented by libraries and the "tradition of the prestige journal" represented by publishers. Schauder's research showed that scholars want both of these fundamentally conflicting traditions retained.

The reputation of the journal or publisher is indeed a key extrinsic attribute, one of the only such attributes, in fact, providing an indication of a publication's value (that is, its intrinsic attributes). That reputation is an important means for scholars and students to determine what to read and in what order. On-line publication in a distributed client-server environment, however, offers us an extrinsic attribute that will serve the same purpose. Indeed, the attribute will be so reliable and direct that it is likely to make us uncomfortable. As in the case of retrospective digital conversion, we should aim to let the scholarly community decide as much as possible for itself what is important. Each item, once in the server, should therefore have attached to it some kind of counter indicating how often the item has been used or accessed (possibly by different groups). Probably most useful to scholars in a particular field would be knowledge of which publications have been accessed not only generally but also by those scholars they consider to belong to their peer group. Special care would need to be taken in devising such a system in order to protect the privacy of the individual. Hyperlinks should also be provided to other sources in which the publication has been cited so that the extent to which the item is cited will be easily apparent. Thus, rather than the potential significance of an item being defined indirectly by its publisher, the item can be determined to be a core publication directly based on the level and type of use it is receiving. The impact of the publication on current scholarship will be in this way at least partially quantified and immediately demonstrable. What a practicing scholar will want to read first is what everyone else in the field is reading, and that will change the sequence in which the scholar and student approach information. This will have implications for their assessment of the literature and their approach to the discipline.

*The specter of bureaucracy.* A recent argument against the institutional model is that "the bureaucratic ineptitude of many large institutions would threaten to become a major barrier to the dissemination of new knowledge—a situation meriting concern" (Lynch, 1993b, p. 15). As a bureaucrat myself, I must admit to a similar apprehension. Of all the objections to the institutional model, this is the one I find most difficult to counter. Private businesses are often able to do things much more efficiently than public organizations such as government agencies or academic institutions. It makes little sense for institutions to assume responsibility for publishing if what is gained by such a radical step is immediately lost to political conflict and poor management. Somehow the work of using (institutional) money to exchange information must be made as efficient as the work (now done by publishers) of using information exchange to make money. If we cannot manage this, then the institutional model admittedly makes little sense and we will need to accept the fact that it is the institution itself that is the real impediment to the creation of an effective scholarly communication system.

**Rescreening.** If the commercial model eventually comes to dominate, the three selection screens will presumably remain in effect although in somewhat different form from what we experience in today's environment. Publishers will continue to undertake the primary screening operation, deciding through their editorial boards which materials to publish. Individual institutions will still provide a secondary screening step because they will not be able to afford to provide their users with access to all of the on-line publications needed. The "collection" will in many ways be shifted in the commercial model from institutions to publishers and we must expect some of the main service responsibilities of libraries to shift to publishers as well. The tertiary screening step (retention decisions) for on-line sources will also shift mainly to publishers and will become therefore all the more problematical because some publishers will presumably only retain the information they own for as long as it is profitable to do so. The fundamental archival role of libraries may therefore be seriously jeopardized. Some agreement would be needed so that publishers either going out of business or seeking to jettison information that is no longer profitable would be prepared or obligated to pass (preferably for free but at least at a fair price) the older information (back) to the academic community for storage. It is at this point that the institutions can exercise their tertiary screening role and decide which older materials they will retain on-line.

If the institutional model is accepted, only two screening operations will exist and they will be entirely different from those of the commercial model. At least in the case of most notification sources, publishing and collection building will merge into a single operation. (I am assuming that many data sources will continue to be published by for-profit publishers. In the institutional model, academic institutions would assume responsibility, from my perspective, primarily for current notification sources.) To add an item to an official institutional server would be simultaneously to publish it and add it to the national collection. This would be the new primary screen. It would be the scholarly community in each discipline that would then decide what is in such a collection. Of course, large quantities of network-accessible information would not be officially published in this way and certainly some groups of scholars would become disgruntled and establish their own servers. The status of such "renegade" servers would need to be determined. Another variation on this theme would be played by scholars who cannot get their material through the primary screen, that is, published in the official disciplinary servers, but who feel their material contributes significantly to the field and therefore decide on self-publication, that is, putting their material on their own servers. This would be more difficult for users to find and such material would normally always be read after that in the official servers but it could still have considerable influence. We must also expect some traffic in preprints, depending on how long editorial boards take to make their decisions, although the heavy use of on-line preprints now in effect in some disciplines should be significantly reduced when all publications are immediately published on-line upon acceptance. The AAU Task Force on "A National Strategy for Managing Scientific and Technical Information" envisions a national on-line repository that consists of two parts, a current collection and one or more permanent collections. The permanent collections would consist of materials that have been subject to peer review; the current collection would be the equivalent of preprints. Any item in the current collection not transferred to the permanent collections in two years would be deleted (Association of American Universities, 1994, pp. 70–71).

**Remembering to Forget.** Information stored on-line will be subject to some physical degradation over time and its accessibility will be in constant jeopardy from hardware and software changes. As a result, a process of what is now called "refreshing" will need to be put into effect: stored information will need to be routinely and periodically recopied if it is to remain accessible (see Kenney and Personius, 1992, pp. 207–08). Preservation in the on-line environment, therefore, is likely to become a fairly automatic process. This will have important financial implications for preservation. It may become more cost-effective in at least the early days of a primarily on-line environment to keep something rather than withdraw it. Withdrawal requires human intervention and decision making; it may be more cost-effective simply to recopy along with the rest of the collection. Eventually, however, the cost of not withdrawing anything will become burdensome. Servers will become overloaded, congested, "noisy," regardless of how sophisticated the technology is, and the user will become increasingly more occupied with finding information than with interpreting and applying it. We will need therefore to learn how to "forget" certain documents, to omit them from the current discussion.

Thus it is likely that libraries will need to develop an entirely new screening method for on-line publications. The question is, do we simply move such publications somehow to one side, in the way we do now through off-site storage, or do we consign such withdrawals to oblivion? (Since there may be only one "copy" of a publication in the national collection, a decision to discard or delete in the on-line environment will often prove irreversible.) The universal utility syndrome will force us in many cases to select the former, that is, to develop a procedure that would still leave the scholar the opportunity to find, albeit with more difficulty, some of the screened-out information. The "difficulty" part is important: while this new tertiary screen need not result in a permanent loss, the recapture of such information should be difficult enough so that only those who truly want it will have the impetus to gain access.

What exactly should we do with such material to downgrade its accessibility? We have already noted that some materials considered less important will probably remain in their original analog form. By the same token, some items that are no longer useful might be converted back into the analog library, that is, transferred to microfilm (still probably the most secure and lowest-maintenance medium) or even printed on acid free paper and stored in a warehouse. They would still be retrievable but in a digital environment such manual access will probably appear so time consuming that the material would appear to most users as virtually lost. Only the largest, most prestigious institutions are likely to maintain such archives and they will be considered well endowed (both financially and informationally) for that reason.

The information congestion that will lead to such tertiary screening may arrive more quickly than we think. We must bear in mind that hypertext as it is now developing has the very real potential to atomize publication. (For a useful, recent introduction to hypertext, see Borman and von Solms, 1993.) Although knowledge and understanding are based on intertextual connections, we are now preparing to establish mechanical systems that create so many connections at such a speed that the result may be not new knowledge but total chaos. The fact that all language and all knowledge are connected becomes a reality through hypertext, which can move the reader from one text to another to another. In some kinds of research, such textual "channel flipping" may be desirable but much other research will require a concentration of attention on a continuous text. The library may need to develop the capacity selectively to disable or restrain those intertextual connections that we have sought for so long to establish. The library should be able to segregate information from the current discussion, to cause the user to forget about it long enough to concentrate on the text at hand. In addition to the process for moving information from digital to analog storage, therefore, some new form of temporary withdrawal may also be needed.

## Conclusion

Rapid advances in information technology present us with an unprecedented opportunity to reenvision and redesign all aspects of scholarly information exchange, including collection building and the scholarly publication process. We must grasp that opportunity, not only to take advantage of the improvements that the new environment will provide but also to apply in that new environment what we have learned—and to correct some of the mistakes we have made—in the old one.

## References

American Physics Society. "Report of the APS Task Force on Electronic Information Systems." *Bulletin of the American Physical Society,* 1991, *36,* 1119–1151.
Association of American Publishers. "An AAP Position Paper on Scanning." Press release, Aug. 5, 1994.
Association of American Universities Research Libraries Project in Collaboration with the Association of Research Libraries. "Reports of the AAU Task Forces on Acquisition and Distribution of Foreign Language and Area Studies Materials, a National Strategy for Managing Scientific and Technological Information, Intellectual Property Rights in an Electronic Environment." Washington, D.C.: Association of Research Libraries, 1994.

Atkinson, R. "Old Forms, New Forms: The Challenge of Collection Development." *College and Research Libraries,* Sept. 1989, *50,* 507–520.

Borman, H., and von Solms, S. H. "Hypermedia, Multimedia, and Hypertext: Definitions and Overview." *Electronic Library,* Aug.–Oct. 1993, *11,* 259–268.

Clarke, R. "Electronic Support for the Practice of Research." *Information Society,* Jan.–Mar. 1994, *10,* 25–42.

Cummings, A. M., Witte, M. L., Bowen, W. G., Lazarus, L. O., and Ekman, R. H. *University Libraries and Scholarly Communication: A Study Prepared for the Andrew W. Mellon Foundation.* Washington, D.C.: Association of Research Libraries, 1992.

Dominguez, P. B., and Swindler, L. "Cooperative Collection Development at the Research Triangle University Libraries: A Model for the Nation." *College and Research Libraries,* Nov. 1993, *54,* 470–496.

Dougherty, R. M. "A 'Factory' for Scholarly Journals." *Chronicle of Higher Education,* June 17, 1992, pp. B1, B3.

Drabenstott, K. M. *Analytical Review of the Library of the Future.* Washington, D.C.: Council on Library Resources, 1994.

Houghton, B. *Scientific Periodicals: Their Historical Development, Characteristics and Control.* London: Clive Bingley, 1975.

James, W. *The Principles of Psychology.* Vol. 1. New York: Henry Holt, 1890.

Kenney, A. R., and Personius, L. K. "The Future of Digital Preservation." *Advances in Preservation and Access,* 1992, *1,* 195–212.

Lanham, R. A. *The Electronic Word: Democracy, Technology, and the Arts.* Chicago: University of Chicago Press, 1993.

Lucier, R. E. "Knowledge Management: Refining Roles in Scientific Communication." *EDUCOM Review,* Fall 1990, *25,* 21–27.

Lucier, R. E. "Toward a Knowledge Management Environment: A Strategic Framework." *EDUCOM Review,* Nov.–Dec. 1992, *27,* 24–31.

Lynch, C. A. "Reaction, Response, and Realization: From the Crisis in Scholarly Communication to the Age of Networked Information." *Serials Review,* Spring/Summer 1992, *18,* 107–112.

Lynch, C. A. "Accessibility and Integrity of Networked Information Collections." Contractor report prepared for the Office of Technology Assessment, 1993a. (NTIS PB93–218923)

Lynch, C. A. "The Transformation of Scholarly Communication and the Role of the Library in the Age of Networked Information." *Serials Librarian,* 1993b, *23,* 5–20.

National Research Council. "National Collaboratories: Applying Information Technology for Scientific Research." Washington, D.C.: National Academy Press, 1993.

Noll, R., and Steinmueller, W. E. "An Economic Analysis of Scientific Journal Prices: Preliminary Results." *Serials Review,* Spring/Summer 1992, *18,* 32–37.

Okerson, A. "With Feathers: Effects of Copyright and Ownership on Scholarly Publishing." *College and Research Libraries,* Sept. 1991, *52,* 425–438.

Rogers, S. J., and Hurt, C. S. "How Scholarly Communication Should Work in the 21st Century." *Chronicle of Higher Education,* Oct. 18, 1989, p. A56. (Reprinted in *College and Research Libraries,* Jan. 1991, *51,* 5–8.)

Rutstein, J. S., DeMiller, A. L., and Fuseler, E. A. "Ownership Versus Access: Shifting Perspectives for Libraries." *Advances in Librarianship,* 1993, *17,* 33–60.

Schauder, D. "Electronic Publishing of Professional Articles: Attitudes of Academics and Implications for the Scholarly Communication Industry." *Journal of the American Association for Information Science,* Mar. 1994, *45,* 73–100.

Stubs, K. "Introduction." *ARL Statistics 1992–93.* Washington, D.C.: Association of Research Libraries, 1994.

*ROSS ATKINSON is associate university librarian at Cornell University in Ithaca, New York.*

*Librarians of the future will be knowledge managers who provide*
*unique skills to students and faculty in the learning-centered campuses*
*of the twenty-first century.*

# The Instructional Program and Responsibilities of the Teaching Library

*Carla J. Stoffle, Karen Williams*

Institutions of higher education must restructure their educational programs and academic support services to be learning-centered rather than teaching-centered, and students must be active participants not passive recipients of the educational program (Guskin, 1994).

To compete effectively in the global information-based economy of the twenty-first century, the United States needs citizen leaders who not only have been educated using the latest knowledge and research in their areas of undergraduate study but also have been prepared to remain lifelong independent learners. As a part of their educational experience, students must gain an understanding of and the ability to use the rapidly evolving information and telecommunication technologies, which will allow for professional and intellectual growth throughout their lifetimes.

All graduates of baccalaureate programs must be able to recognize when they need information, what kind of information they need, and where to look for it to complete a task successfully. They must also be able to do this effectively regardless of the information's format, source, or location. They must understand how information is structured and organized and how the structure, organization, availability, and retrievability of information are influenced by the structure and organization of the dominant society. Students must master the basic skills needed to manipulate the vast and growing amount of information including full text, images, video, sound, hypermedia, numerical data, and citations, which will continue to be retrievable twenty-four hours a day through local, regional, national, and international networks. They must develop an awareness and understanding of information policy issues, such as privacy, copyright, intellectual property, privatization of government information, information pricing, and access and universal service. Furthermore, they must be able to relate to how these policy issues interact with and affect society, the social structure, mass media, and the global economy. In short, graduates from our colleges and universities must be "information literate" (American Library Association, 1989).

For most colleges and universities, this is a mandate to provide students with a learning environment that incorporates state of the art information and telecommunication technologies into instructional programs, that removes the educational barriers of time and place that are a part of the traditional classroom and the information-seeking process.

At the center of this technological change on the campus and key to the success of the institution in creating the new learning environment is a restructured academic library. The transformed library will be one that does the following:

Focuses on teaching as both a direct activity and a support activity for other disciplines

Creates new knowledge packages and access tools

Provides a physical environment that facilitates student and faculty research and collaboration

Provides access to resources that are the necessary underpinnings of the new learning environment and learning activities.

The new library will be a place where personnel and facilities are available to support faculty in the creation of digitized teaching materials. It will provide laboratory space for faculty and student experimentation with advanced technology and software, it will enable students to work in groups, and it will include facilities for electronic publishing and printing.

All services will be customer-based, relying on research data that define information needs and use characteristics. Continuous improvement of services and programs will be a priority. The goal of the library will be to foster self-sufficiency among users and to create lifelong, self-directed learners. The new academic library will be a teaching library (Guskin and others, 1979; Stoffle and others, 1984; Tompkins, 1990).

Before describing the new teaching library and looking into the array of its activities, we will explore why the library is central to the transformation of the campus learning environment and describe the current state of the instructional programs and library services at most institutions today. The last section in the chapter discusses both what is necessary to achieve the library's transformation and the way in which it is likely to occur.

## Why the Library?

The library is central to the successful restructuring of the undergraduate education program because information is the library's primary business. The selection, organization, dissemination, storage, preservation, and management of information are the library's traditional domain. Teaching how to find, use, and evaluate information is the responsibility of librarians.

A major investment exists in the infrastructure of the library and in the organizational expertise to deal with information problems and issues. In general, academic libraries and librarians have done a good job in managing the institution's investment. Basic library programs and services that support the transition and new learning-centered curriculum are in place, even if they have not been systematized or are not as successful as they need to be.

The integral nature of the library's involvement in the transformation process is also indicated by the relationship between it and the faculty and their academic values. Of all support and information services, the library is the most academic. Librarians are most likely to be considered peers by the faculty. Library-faculty relationships have been nurtured over many years. Libraries have a close and special understanding of the research and instructional needs of the institution. Librarians share the academic values that drive the campus. They share the classroom with faculty in providing general instruction on use of library resources, including the new on-line systems and the Internet. They have educated and organized themselves to serve individual disciplines or groups of disciplines. They understand how the literatures of different disciplines are organized and accessed by scholars. In sum, librarians are academic colleagues who already work easily with and carry innovations to the faculty.

In addition, on most campuses the library was among the first academic units to experience the effects of the new information technologies. For most units, the application of the technologies has been to automate current work. The library went through this stage; librarians now use the technologies to do new and different things that were made possible only through the new technologies. Librarians have also developed close working relationships with other information professionals. This combination of expertise and ability to work with other key information players provides them with the ability and credibility to take leadership roles in the campus transformation.

## Current Situation in Higher Education

In most cases, individual faculty members in individual courses have used technology to transform or improve education with little or no commitment from the institution and little institutionwide impact. Although many campuses are in the process of investing in the voice, data, and image networks and the hardware for faculty, students, and classrooms that will make educational transformation possible, few have made a commitment to the concept of the learning-centered curriculum or have the necessary infrastructure to make it happen.

The staff of the library and the computer center, media technology services, and other services provide educational support services for faculty members who wish to achieve their goals. They offer consulting services to faculty and sponsor workshops about the tools and the facilities for both faculty and students. In the library, instruction in how to find and use information to complete a specific course assignment is often provided. In some instances, librarians work with faculty to structure assignments to ensure that the content learning objective is achieved at the same time that information retrieval skills are learned. In other instances, librarians deal with more general information literacy issues. Separate credit courses taught by librarians or team-taught by librarians and faculty are offered sporadically, usually in institutions where the library's commitment to education and the faculty's receptivity to information literacy instruction are combined. However, these educational efforts are not systematic or sufficient to create a learning-centered university and a restructured curriculum. This kind of instruction is reactive. It makes little impact outside of the particular course. Teaching information literacy skills and working with faculty to improve the learning environment is currently neither a top priority of the library nor of the institution for the library.

There are exceptions. One exciting development is the National Learning Infrastructure Initiative (NLII), a coalition of higher education institutions, businesses, and associations sponsored by Educom. The group seeks national systemic change for higher education and advocates the creation of a reengineered, learning-centered environment, emphasizing the need for an infrastructure to facilitate learning through technology. The forty-six founding NLII members include Indiana University; Maricopa County Community College District; Miami-Dade Community College; University of California, Berkeley; University of Iowa; University of Michigan; and University of Minnesota (Educom, n.d.). These institutions expect to provide models and insights based on their own experiences to those that wish to follow.

The Minnesota State University system has created a plan that recognizes information literacy as the underlying principle of undergraduate education for the next century and identifies the library as a critical force in graduating information-literate citizens. The plan provides a framework for redesigning the physical library as a teaching library (Jones, 1992).

Some libraries are restructuring services in order to help lead their campuses in the creation of new learning-centered programs. Some are creating new access tools and innovative knowledge management packages. Among them are the academic libraries at the University of Southern California; the University of Washington; the University of Iowa; the University of Arizona; Northwestern University; Johns Hopkins Medical School; the University of California, San Francisco; Cornell; the Massachusetts Institute of Technology; the University of Michigan; Ohio State University; Cleveland State University; Case Western Reserve; Wayne State University; the University of Louisville; Purdue University; Rice University; Bradley University; Earlham College; and Gettysburg College.

Some academic libraries are working together to create models through the Coalition for Networked Information Working Group on Teaching and Learning. This group held a conference entitled "Creating New Learning Communities Via the Network" at Estrella Mountain Community College in August 1994. In attendance were teams from ten institutions who have introduced information technologies to foster collaboration among faculty, students, librarians, and computing professionals to improve course content and the teaching and learning process. The purpose of the session was to help these libraries further their own efforts and to provide models for others (Peters, 1994).

## The Teaching Library

The new teaching library, which will focus on users and their needs, will be directly involved in and provide support for teaching, research, and service on the campus of the future. No two libraries are likely to have the exact same programs, organizational structure, or physical arrangement. However, what they will have in common across academic institution types and over time will be the following goals:

Creating an information-literate undergraduate
Supporting and facilitating a learning-centered curriculum and research programs for specific disciplines
Improving the quality of teaching materials and assignments
Improving campus understanding of and participation in local and information policy development
Providing access to information, knowledge, and physical facilities
Conducting research and evaluation to improve programs and advance knowledge about and access to information.

**Education.** Creating lifelong independent learners will be at the heart of all activities. The librarian's primary duty must be to teach and structure independent and collaborative learning experiences. To do so, well-planned programs and a specific curriculum will be needed. The library need not offer separate credit courses although these might be used. Instead, activities should be included in required core or general education courses in conjunction with a series of discipline-specific courses that is team-taught by faculty and librarians. Knowledge and skills may also be learned through computer, audiovisual, or printed instructional packages, and through workshops designed and offered by the library. Ultimately, the delivery mechanism is unimportant, as long as the learning is systematic and the product is graduates who are able to function as self-sufficient, self-directed learners throughout their lifetimes.

Librarians will all be required to teach faculty how to use the new information technologies in their subject courses and create learning experiences and tools that engage students and make them active participants in the educational process. Librarians already have some experience in this sort of thing through their activities in helping faculty design assignments with print-based information tools. In the future, however, it will be necessary to go beyond helping faculty know what is available and how to use it as librarians and others participate in the actual design of new packages and tools. To improve instruction as it is being delivered, they will help develop evaluation and feedback mechanisms. For example, it will be possible to design assignments using actual NASA data, climatological and environmental data sets, or data collected from social sciences studies. It will be possible for students to do a text analysis of an author's original work or analyze famous paintings, photographs, or other works of art using electronic access to collections all over the world. A possible group project might be to conduct spatial analyses using several data sets and then create maps that visualize new relationships. Video and audio materials are increasingly available in digitized form. Students will be able to access and use these in multimedia presentations to replace or supplement term papers and traditional student speeches or class presentations.

The UWIRED experiment at the University of Washington is an excellent example of how librarians are working with both faculty and computing professionals to integrate information technology into instruction. Participating faculty and teaching assistants took a five-day crash course led by librarians and computing and communications staff members. The course included such topics as how to integrate Internet and E-mail into classroom teaching and take-home assignments and how to use library data bases in the classroom. As part of the project, a team of librarians is teaching a required two-credit technology seminar, with discipline-specific instruction on electronic resources and their applications in the classroom. Students are introduced to electronic mail, on-line discussion groups, the Internet, data base searching, and the sociopolitical issues surrounding the use of computer technology. They have access to a model classroom in the undergraduate library, with computers attached to the campus network, and each student receives a laptop computer for use during the project. The seminar culminates with students collaborating on the creation of a multimedia project designed to integrate skills learned throughout the year (Monaghan, 1994; Mudrock, 1994).

The Information Arcade at the University of Iowa is another example of collaboration among the university libraries, the Office of Information Technology, and the academic faculty to improve instruction and create information-literate students. This elaborate facility, housed in the library, was designed to support the use of electronic resources in research, teaching, and independent learning. The Information Arcade consists of an electronic classroom, a separate group of information stations for individual use, a cluster of multimedia stations, a course preparation lab, and an information desk. The arcade places emphasis on the following (Lowry, 1994, p. 40):

Using nonbibliographic electronic source materials, including electronic texts, image, and multimedia data bases, numeric data, and courseware
Analyzing, manipulating, and creating information in electronic format using information access and management tools, software for analysis and simulation, and programs for multimedia authoring and for collaborative work

Integrating computer-based resources and techniques into the undergraduate and graduate curricula and into library instruction
Providing expert, in-depth information and instructional services to support computer-aided teaching, learning, and research.

More than forty academic classes met in the electronic classroom during its first year. In a particularly innovative literature course, rather than writing term papers students created their own multimedia projects on an aspect of the Columbian World Exposition of 1893. Students were inspired by the large multimedia data base created by the professor and excited by the open-ended nature of the assignment. They used a variety of resources including scanners, software, E-mail, the Internet, and printed books. In the words of one student, "We have the opportunity—the responsibility—to add to a large, growing base of information . . . to illuminate the previous data in a nontrivial way!" (Lowry, 1994, p. 42).

The University of Southern California's teaching library is a new undergraduate library facility that is committed to creating users who can use materials in any format. It houses a center for scholarly technology, special classrooms for teaching use of the new information technologies, seminar rooms with acoustical control and full network capability, and labs where faculty can design new instructional tools. The library has also re-created the traditional reference area into an "Information Commons," which houses both print and electronic materials and is staffed by librarians and computer personnel. Students work on their information problems in groups of two or three working at oversized computer workstations. The library is open twenty-four hours a day.

**Knowledge Management.** In teaching libraries, the library is no longer merely a storehouse or gateway for information produced elsewhere, but a place where new knowledge packages and new access tools are created specifically to enhance teaching and research. This activity is called *knowledge management*. It involves structuring works as they are created so that they are maximally accessible. It includes creating ways of accessing existing resources to enable the highest level of integration with the client's work. It is a system that brings together hardware, software, control mechanisms, on-line resources, and human expertise in ways that help to create new knowledge and that produce highly relevant search results that match users' information gathering and usage patterns (Gapen, Hampton, and Schmitt, 1993). The knowledge management environment is characterized by complex, high-quality, dynamic data bases that are critical to daily work; integrated electronic systems and services; on-line tools to collaboratively build, maintain, share, and use data bases; and interface tools for access to multiple local and remote data bases (Gapen, Hampton, and Schmitt, 1993, p. 26).

As part of their daily work, librarians will create, with faculty and other information professionals, new knowledge products that will go beyond merely digitizing information in books and journals. New access tools and the creation of electronic pointers to the location of information will be the responsibility of staff who formerly cataloged and processed physical additions to the collections.

**Information Provision.** Just as the classroom lecture has been the standard instructional methodology for decades, the reference desk has been the focal point for information provision in libraries. In the teaching library, reference services will be reconceptualized as information provision services. The reorganization will encompass the traditional reference desk but go far beyond it.

Emphasis will be placed on the overall organization, management, and use of information and information systems, with librarians interfacing between information technology, producers of information, and users of information. Everything from collection arrangement and signage to data base construction and software design will be undertaken with the self-sufficient client in mind. Tools such as on-line help guides available around the clock and information kiosks designed to handle directional or repetitive questions will provide valuable information at the point of need and reduce the amount of time that librarians spend interpreting poorly designed systems.

As new technologies encourage remote use of on-line catalogs and other information resources, teaching libraries will offer corresponding remote information services. Although libraries have offered telephone service for many years, it has usually been assigned a lower priority than serving clients who are physically in the building.

Information services are no longer location-specific. Similarly, librarians and clients are no longer limited to the resources owned by the library. The "teledesk" is likely to become a new means of providing information services. Clients will approach a television screen that may be located anywhere and, using interactive telecommunications technology, consult with a librarian who may be across the campus or in another city or state. After consultation, the librarian may display information on the screen or transmit files directly to the client's own computer. Thus, "reference" is redefined as a national cooperative information provision service, eliminating the need for the consultant and the client to be at the same location (Creth, 1993, p. 129). With this kind of interinstitutional cooperation it will no longer be necessary for every campus library to hire local experts in all disciplines. Librarians in the future will also have a more proactive role in information provision. The librarian will be vested in personalizing information and providing knowledge in the context of the recipient's interests (Murr and Williams, 1987, p. 11). Through assessment and connection development activities, which are described in the next section, they will profile the information needs of individuals and academic departments. As part of the research team, librarians will add value by selecting, analyzing, and synthesizing information that will then be delivered electronically.

**Connection Development.** Reaching out to the campus community to share information about the library is an activity in which libraries have engaged for many years. Lectures, exhibits, and other cultural programs to highlight the collections and stimulate intellectual growth among students and faculty are offered to some extent by almost all of them. In teaching libraries, activities go beyond the one-way communication represented by traditional outreach activities. Termed *connection development,* the activity involves creating partnerships—connections or two-way communication—to advance information provision, knowledge, information policy development, and intellectual growth and development for the campus community. Librarians move out of the library and away from service desks. They interact with faculty and students on their own "turf" and actively seek to build productive relationships. Meaningful dialog and communication are ongoing activities, not actions taken only when the library has a budget problem or wants support for a potentially unpopular change. Through connection development librarians stimulate dialog about, understanding of, and actions for solving information policy and scholarly communication process issues on an ongoing basis. These kinds of issues have the potential for profound impact on the educational program and faculty research. Effective institutional participation on state and national levels requires that these and other information issues be seen as institutional problems and not as library problems.

**Information Resource Development and Preservation.** In the teaching library and the restructured learning-centered university, the quality of learning will be even more dependent on the quality of the resources that support it than it is today. Therefore, information resource development and preservation activities will continue to be important activities for librarians. Decisions about what to put physically on the shelves, what to mount on local systems, which data bases to subscribe to, which resources to share with other libraries, and what information to purchase will be critical. Librarians also will need to make decisions about which local materials they wish to preserve using digital technologies and which of these they wish to make available over local and national networks.

For information access decisions to be made effectively, librarians will work closely with faculty. They will have data about the national availability and use of materials by discipline as well as on local program needs and characteristics. Librarians also will manage the resources allocated for the information needs of the discipline for which they are responsible rather than have centrally managed information and budgets.

The structure of the information budget will also change. Interlibrary loan and document delivery costs, and the increasing costs of on-line electronic sources and the conversion of images and text to digital form, will need to be included. Publishing and on-demand printing of materials will also become a part of the information budget.

**Assessment.** Librarians will spend considerable time in assessment activities. Data about user requirements are needed in order to plan programs and ensure that they effectively meet the highest priority needs of the users. All programmatic decisions will be based on data. Customer satisfaction and a library's outputs or products will become the measure of library effectiveness rather than the input—dollars spent, size of staff, numbers of books purchased, and so on.

## Transition to the Teaching Library

**What the Library Needs to Do.** Thus, the shift to the teaching library requires a shift in emphasis to users and their needs. To create self-sufficient information-literate users the library has to concentrate on outcomes. Staff must change from material processing roles to direct user contact roles and to the creation of access and knowledge management tools. Organizational structures must be flattened with staff organized into teams that reflect the campus organization and structure. The personnel in the teaching library must be empowered to meet needs as they arise. They must be risk takers. They must be continuous learners, staying at the cutting edge of technology, if they are to design new access systems and knowledge packages. Time and resources must be made available to help them grow and develop. This includes both formal education and development programs and time to "play" with the new technologies and learn to be creative with them.

Many library personnel will experience substantial anxiety and discomfort in the switch to the teaching library. Individuals who have performed competently in the traditional library environment will find it difficult to change their work style and priorities. Continuous learning takes time and energy. Working in teams effectively is hard. Staff will likely experience burnout and stress until new structures that enable them to influence and direct their work lives are in place.

Today's personnel and compensation policies and procedures will be inadequate for the needs of the teaching library. Narrow job descriptions will work against the effective functioning of teams and personal growth. Merit compensation programs will maintain individualism and competitiveness rather than the cooperation needed for flexible, high performing work groups.

Focusing on the needs of the campus user will require that librarians change the cycle time for designing and introducing new services. Currently, libraries implement new services once every few years. In the new environment this would be unresponsive to changing user needs. New services and library innovations will have to be introduced at a rate of at least two or three annually.

To achieve its goals, the library will no longer be self-sufficient. Programs will require partnerships, coalitions, and close coordination, perhaps even new organizational structures. A team of information professionals with technical expertise and knowledge of users, information organization, and systems will be needed to create and maintain new systems. Coordination and cooperation with instructional design specialists—teaching center and faculty development personnel—will also be needed. Alliances with bookstore, university press, and printing and publishing personnel will have to be actively maintained if the necessary instructional support products are to be created. Partnerships with vendors of library services and materials and other academic institutions will also have to be created. No single institution will be able to do everything needed. This will bring exciting opportunities and new creativity (and, potentially, new resources) to institutions but it will also force them to interact with outside constituencies on an ongoing basis.

For the teaching library to be effective, library space will also need to be rethought. Today's physical library will not disappear. In addition to housing the continued acquisition of print, multimedia, software, and other such materials, the library will need to offer a teaching center where faculty can work with information professionals to design new instructional materials. Also needed will be areas where students can work collaboratively in group settings. Indeed, the teaching library facilities will need considerable and ongoing upgrading. Reference areas will have to be completely redesigned with large study tables that accommodate electronic workstations, printers, and fax machines as well as printed materials. Electrical and telecommunications wiring will need to be installed throughout so that there is access to the network from virtually any location in the library. Then, multimedia classroom facilities will have to be kept up to date for instruction in all the new technologies. And buildings will need to be flexible to allow adjustment as technologies change.

The cost of the shift to the teaching library will be substantial. Some of the resources will have to come from within the library through reallocation and implementation of process improvement projects to gain savings. Libraries will have to scrutinize their activities and give up those of lesser value. However, the campus will also have to commit new resources: the library budget will have to be restructured to accommodate and support the new priorities and demands. More money may go to staffing and providing access to information than to the purchase of physical items.

**What University Administrators Need to Do.**  Creating a learning-centered campus requires a substantial initial investment that will not generate dividends in the short term. Much has to change and the changes will be hard to make. Faculty must be trained both intellectually and emotionally for their new instructional roles and support structures must be put in place to help them make the transition. Traditional organizational structures have to be broken down. New partnerships and coalitions do not just happen; they must be nurtured. Academic support personnel will have to develop new skills and priorities. The campus has to be completely wired. There must be personnel to maintain systems and support the technology. In addition, money must be available to refresh and upgrade equipment on an ongoing basis.

Administrative leadership, vision, and ability will be needed to stay the course under pressure. Administrators must ask the right questions, such as, Where are we going and how can information technology help? How can we best organize our information resources and technologies to make the strongest contribution to the identified priorities? How can we best deploy our human and fiscal information technology resources so that all graduates are information literate? (Breivik, 1994). Setting clear goals and removing bureaucratic constraints so that all units can use their resources to meet those goals will be a necessary activity. Creating an environment that encourages risk taking and innovation and minimizes the penalty for mistakes will be key.

The teaching library can only be created under these conditions. The risks that the library will take to eliminate activities with less value and move away from a collection-centered focus will be enormous. Most faculty have a strong commitment to their collections and many have unique service requirements that, if eliminated, will cause substantial unhappiness. Furthermore, the time commitment needed to create the necessary skills and structure for supporting the teaching library may mean that in the short term services not only do not improve but actually decline.

University administrators must also take the time to understand what the teaching library is about. They must know what to look for and then follow up with these activities and programs.

Library administrators will require substantial support from senior university administrators to deal with the unhappiness of staff and faculty. Such support must be reflected in regular public acknowledgment that the library is taking the direction the campus wishes. Organizational red tape and barriers, especially in the personnel management and administrative areas of the university, will have to be removed. Financial support will be important. Finally, library administrators will need some emotional support, including personal expressions of confidence in their competence.

## Conclusion

Institutions of higher education are facing both great challenges and unprecedented opportunity. Preparing the leaders of the next century requires fundamental changes in our undergraduate education programs. Learning-centered education and information literacy are requirements, not options. The academic library as teaching library not only is central to the successful transformation of the educational program but also can provide the leadership to help the rest of the institution make the necessary changes.

## References

American Library Association Presidential Committee on Information Literacy. *Final Report.* Chicago: American Library Association, 1989.

Breivik, P. S. "Investing Wisely in Information Technology: Asking the Right Questions." *CAUSE/EFFECT,* 1994, *17* (3), 47–50.

Creth, S. D. "Creating a Virtual Information Organization: Collaborative Relationships Between Libraries and Computing Centers." *Journal of Library Administration,* 1993, *19* (3–4), 111–132.

Educom. *NLII Call to Participate.* (Brochure.) Washington, D.C.: Educom, n.d.

Gapen, D. K., Hampton, Q., and Schmitt, S. "TQM: The Director's Perspective." *Journal of Library Administration,* 1993, *18* (1–2), 15–28.

Guskin, A. E. "Reducing Student Costs and Enhancing Student Learning, Part II: Restructuring the Role of Faculty." *Change,* Sept.–Oct. 1994, pp. 16–25.

Guskin, A. E., Stoffle, C. J., and Boisse, J. A. "The Academic Library as a Teaching Library: A Role for the 1980s." *Library Trends,* 1979, *28* (2), 281–296.

Jones, L. B. "Linking Undergraduate Education and Libraries: Minnesota's Approach." In D. W. Farmer and T. F. Mech (eds.), *Information Literacy: Developing Students as Independent Learners.* New Directions for Higher Education, no. 78. San Francisco: Jossey-Bass, 1992.

Lowry, A. K. "The Information Arcade at the University of Iowa." *CAUSE/EFFECT,* 1994, *17* (3), 38–44.

Monaghan, P. "Powering Up the Students." *Chronicle of Higher Education,* Nov. 9, 1994, pp. A19–A20.

Mudrock, T. "UWIRED: Creating an Electronic Learning Community." *Library Directions/A Newsletter of the University of Washington Libraries,* 1994, *5* (1), 2.

Murr, L. E., and Williams, J. B. "The Roles of the Future Library." *Library Hi Tech,* 1987, *5* (3), 7–23.

Peters, P. E. "Creating New Learning Communities Via the Network: Coalition for Networked Information Holds Conference." (Electronic file.) CNI-ANNOUNCE listserv, Aug. 1994.

Stoffle, C. J., Guskin, A. E., and Boisse, J. A. "Teaching, Research, and Service: The Academic Library's Role." In T. G. Kirk (ed.), *Increasing the Teaching Role of Academic Librarians.* New Directions for Teaching and Learning, no. 18. San Francisco: Jossey-Bass, 1984.

Tompkins, P. "New Structures for Teaching Libraries: Goals and Objectives for USC's New Library." *Library Administration and Management,* 1990, *4,* 77–81.

*CARLA J. STOFFLE is dean of libraries at the University of Arizona Library.*

*KAREN WILLIAMS is social sciences team leader at the University of Arizona Library.*

*The technology revolution and the information explosion are raising
revolutionary issues not only for the library but also for the very
process of learning. The accrediting process should be a vehicle for
moving exploration of these issues into the center of the institution.*

# Using the Accreditation Process to Transform the Mission of the Library

*Ralph A. Wolff*

The process of institutional self-study, evaluation visit, and team report, which
forms the core of the accreditation process, is a uniquely American one. The
periodic opportunity to assess institutional strengths and weaknesses can lead
to insights, plans for improvement, and institutional and program change.
Occasionally, self-study linked with a team visit can lead to fundamental, even
transformative changes. There is an opportunity now to use the accrediting
process to stimulate fundamental rethinking of the mission, role, and operation of the library.

The convergence of the technological revolution and the information
explosion are already having a dramatic impact on all academic libraries. All
regional accrediting associations have adopted standards or criteria for the
review of the libraries and information resources of accredited institutions.
Yet none are equal to the emerging needs of higher education and our increasingly information-based society. Ironically, the process of accreditation self-
study is one of the best vehicles for campus leaders outside and within
libraries to use to develop the foundation for change within the institution.
Unlike separate library planning documents, the self-study is reviewed by a
team of outside evaluators who can validate and influence the future direction of the library by writing findings and recommendations about the library
and its relationship to the institution to external constituencies. Moreover, the
accreditation process provides a clear opportunity for campus leaders to bring
together library staff, faculty, and others and for the library evaluation to be
placed in the context of the institution as a whole. This chapter explores the
approaches used by regional accrediting commissions, analyzes the organizing principles that underlie our understanding of libraries within the broader

institution, and suggests new approaches to be used by libraries in conducting self-studies.

## Current Accrediting Approach

**Overview of Accrediting Standards.** Six of the seven regional accrediting commissions have adopted formal standards for the review of libraries and learning resource centers. (Although there are six regions, one regional association, the Western Association of Schools and Colleges, has two higher education commissions, one for community and junior colleges and the other for four-year and graduate institutions.) Two excellent reviews of the standards used by each of these associations are found in Garten (1994, pp. 141–155) and Coleman and Jarred (1994, pp. 273–284). Their analyses show that the approach of all to libraries is based on traditional criteria of resources and inputs.

Common regional standards deal with holdings, physical facilities, staffing, budgets, and access. Through revisions over the past decade, more attention has been placed on off-campus programs as well, with attention to resources and service at all sites where educational programs are offered. More recently, greater attention has been placed on library usage and outcomes assessment of the library, though Coleman and Jarred correctly point out that the current construction of library quality indicators still emphasizes inputs over outcomes (p. 276). The Middle States Association has been the most active in promoting information literacy as part of the accrediting process and states in its standards: "Each institution should facilitate optimal use of its learning resources through a variety of strategies designed to help students develop information literacy—the ability to locate, evaluate and use information and to become independent learners" (Middle States Association of Colleges and Schools, 1992, p. 17).

**Library Self-Studies and Evaluation Reports.** Recent reviews of accreditation self-studies and team reports conducted by Leach (1992) in the north central region and by this author in the western region (Wolff, 1994, p. 127) support the conclusion that resources and inputs still dominate. Only infrequently do the self-study and evaluation team report advance issues or identify evidence that could lead to new thinking about the library.

**Need for a New Model.** As I have urged elsewhere (Wolff, 1992, p. 450; Wolff, 1994, pp. 126–127), evaluation of the library needs to include the following issues: the library's relationship to the mission of the institution, the effectiveness of the library in accomplishing its mission, the role of the library in program review and course development, and the connection of the library to emerging efforts of institutions to assess student learning. Ultimately, there is a need for the library to be challenged to develop data that link it more closely to the educational and learning enterprise of the institution.

**Organizing Principles.** Exhortations for "new approaches" to self-study do not, in and of themselves, lead to change. Experience with hundreds of institutions and visiting teams involved in the accrediting process suggest that as time pressure builds to complete a written report—self-study or site-visit team—there is an inevitable reversion to traditional indicators of quality. Developing new approaches to self-study and team evaluation requires significant preplanning and conceptual development, especially in the identification of appropriate quality indicators and the generation and analysis of qualitative and quantitative data. A powerful device for exploring new approaches to self-study is to reflect on the organizing principles behind the questions asked. Organizing principles refer to the values and mental models that shape our thinking and fundamental patterns of organization. Such an exercise can reveal deeply embedded assumptions, often implicit, about how quality is defined in our institutions and help determine which principles continue to serve our needs and which may no longer be effective. For example, consider four organizing principles that could be used to address quality at an institution or library: resources, research, students, and learning. Quality indicators vary significantly under each one. Consequently, questions asked or data collected under each one could also differ dramatically, leading to very different planning processes, self-studies, or team visits. Table 6.1 illustrates this concept.

The indicators shown reflect the efforts of many librarians, faculty, and staff members who have attempted to explore how different organizing principles can affect their approach to self-study. Although still in a preliminary state, the work has demonstrated that one can organize a self-study, ask questions, and collect data about many topics and still not be clear about the mission of the library or its connection to student learning. Experience has also shown that it is relatively easy to develop indicators for the first three principles. But when discussions are drawn to what constitutes proper indicators for student learning, especially for the library, it is difficult.

Yet a library's effectiveness must be addressed in terms of the organizing principle. A library might be highly effective according to resource or research indicators but unable to demonstrate how it contributes to student learning. Conversely, a library could prove its impact on students and learning but be seen to be underfunded by traditional resource indicators. In addition, high student satisfaction may (or may not) be linked to any evidence of student learning. That is, satisfaction with the hours of operation, library environment, and the friendliness of library staff may not assure that students have learned needed information literacy skills.

Going through this exercise at the outset of a self-study process can yield many positive benefits, helping not only to identify what the participants consider appropriate quality indicators but also to reveal hidden assumptions about organizing principles.

## Building an Effective Culture of Evidence

Most libraries already have a considerable stockpile of data, much of it regularly collected and used in discussions of library quality and needs. As the

### Table 6.1. Four Organizing Principles

| Organizing Principle | Indicators of Institutional Quality | Indicators of Library Quality |
| --- | --- | --- |
| 1. Resources | Size of endowment, budget<br>Size and qualifications of faculty<br>Selectivity of student body<br>Size and condition of physical plant<br>Number of computer labs | Size of budget, endowment<br>Size and compensation of staff<br>Size and variety of collections<br>Square footage of library; number of seats<br>Number of computers and CD-ROM players |
| 2. Research | Research productivity of faculty<br>Research dollars generated<br><br>Budget to support research<br><br>Research development activities | Reference staff, budget<br>Reference inquiries of students and faculty<br>Number and type of indexing and abstracting tools<br>Offerings of bibliographic instruction |
| 3. Students | Student selectivity<br>Attrition and retention rates<br>Placement statistics<br>Alumni satisfaction<br>Availability of student services<br>Student-to-faculty ratio | Number of students served<br>Student satisfaction<br>Hours of facilities<br>Timeliness of access<br>Cost of services<br>Availability of duplicate resources |
| 4. Learning | Basic skill levels: writing, numeracy<br>Critical thinking skills<br><br>Lifelong learning skills<br><br>Major field proficiency<br><br>Institution and program goals | Effectiveness of bibliographic instruction<br>Contribution to students' critical thinking skills<br>Lifelong use of information resources<br>Ability to generate researchable questions<br>Library learning goals |

foregoing discussion attempted to illustrate, however, it is not always clear that such data cover the most important issues or are used appropriately in an assessment. An important dimension to the accreditation process is the opportunity it affords to determine whether the library is asking the right questions, collecting useful data, analyzing the data effectively, disseminating the data to those who can benefit, and relying upon data effectively for decision making and improvement. These are all elements of a "culture of evidence," where qualitative and quantitative evidence is used to inform decision making and efforts to improve institution, program, or unit performance. Accrediting associations are placing more emphasis on assessment and outcomes data and this is beginning to affect the evaluation process for libraries.

Unfortunately, most publications on assessment authored by nonlibrarians do not link issues of effective assessment for libraries with broader institutional assessment efforts. A review of several recently published books on assessment, as well as periodicals and occasional papers dealing with institutional assessment, consistently ignore library, learning technology, or information literacy issues. When mentioned, libraries are discussed in terms of meeting resource or access goals but they are rarely linked to the assessment of learning goals for students. An outcome of the self-study process should be the improvement of the infrastructure for assessment of the library so that after the process is completed, improved and more useful data are regularly collected and analyzed.

## Rethinking the Library's Fundamental Role

One of the most exciting opportunities presented by the self-study process is to allow library leaders to collaborate with others throughout the institution to explore the library's mission in relationship to the institution. The converging technology revolution and knowledge explosion make revision of its mission a necessity and provide a basis for its emerging, fundamentally different role. In many ways, the scope and character of the changes under way in the library rise to the level of a "paradigm shift" popularized by Kuhn (1970).

**Newtonian Model.** A metaphor for the impending change may be found in the shift from Newtonian to quantum physics. In Newtonian physics, the universe was seen as a machine, a set of parts or objects that functioned well together. We learned about the universe by taking things apart and studying them. The assumption was that an understanding of the whole is obtained by studying each of the parts (Wheatley, 1993). In science, this system has been enormously effective in discovering principles of parts. We could not have the bridges and roads and lifestyle we have today without understanding the laws of objects. But, as we all know, the number of parts to study is infinite, and we are now moving farther and farther from the center, from any sense of the whole, by a preoccupation with the parts.

The notion that the world is made up of parts has fundamentally affected the concept and structure of higher education. Learning has historically been viewed as knowledge or mastery of facts about parts. We divide the world into disciplines to study parts. We then divide the study of the discipline into parts called courses. A person is learned or "educated" based on the ability to master one of the "parts" that we call a major. Reich (1992) describes how this thinking created the assembly line not only in industry but also in education. Courses are designed to be taken in linear fashion and when a certain number have been taken and their credits accumulated, the person graduates. We presume that the student can put the pieces together into a coherent whole. Even when rare attempts are made to form bridges between parts, they still represent an accumulation of knowledge about parts rather than about the whole.

The Newtonian approach deeply affects everything we do, think, and value, and the way in which we structure the world around us, including higher education. Thus student services are commonly separated from academics and the library functions as a separate entity, although always looking for connections with other parts of the institution. The library not only is physically separate but also functions as an independent unit with separate staffs, budgets, priorities, and so on. Librarians frequently express concern about their separation from the central academic enterprise of their institutions despite the rhetoric about their centrality to the educational mission of the institution.

Moreover, the essential purpose of libraries, even as we move into the information age, is to serve primarily the Newtonian worldview. Libraries are organized to accumulate information about the parts, preserve the historical record about the parts, and support learning that focuses on the parts. Thus, the library's hopeless task is always to attempt to keep up with the increasing creation of more and more parts to study and more and more records to accumulate about each of the parts. This system is rapidly breaking down. No faculty can offer courses about all the parts or even all of the elements that we now know about the single part that we call a discipline. We compromise and never feel satisfied that we are giving our students enough information, let alone a sense of the whole.

**Impact of Technology and the Knowledge Explosion.** Libraries are bursting with the fiscal and physical difficulties of developing current and comprehensive collections to serve disciplines that are growing exponentially. As access to technology and new bibliographic data bases increase, library costs are increasing, dashing our hope that technology would become a "quick fix" for the financial constraints libraries face (Wolff and Steadman, 1994).

It is hard for any of us to comprehend the scale of the knowledge explosion. As Appleberry (1992) describes it: "The sum total of humankind's knowledge doubled from 1750 to 1900. It doubled again from 1900 to 1950. It doubled again from 1950 to 1960. Again from 1960 to 1965. It has been estimated that the sum total of humankind's knowledge has doubled at least once every five years since. . . . It is further projected that by the year 2020, knowledge will double every seventy-three days!"

Because of this knowledge explosion the model under which libraries function and even the model of learning that universities apply no longer work. Accrediting associations contribute to this outdated mode of thinking by focusing on the parts of an institution and on the parts of library function without addressing the implications for the whole. Separate standards for libraries that focus on holdings size, budgets, staff, and facilities no longer make sense. They must be linked to the educational purpose of the institution as a whole.

**Expanding the "Idea" of the Library.** To address the enormous technological changes caused by on-line catalogs, bibliographic and full-text data bases, and telecommunications and the additional consequences of the knowledge explosion, the "idea" of the library has been shifting. The following list, expanding on the work of Martell (1991), highlights the time frame and character of the shift.

| Time | Paradigm |
|------|----------|
| Before 1980 | Holdings |
| 1980 | Access |
| 1995 | Use |
| 2010 | Learning transformation |

The traditional role of the library is that of an archive of the collected wisdom of civilization. Pelikan (1992, p. 118), quoting John Henry Newman, characterizes the university library as "an embalming of past genius" and, in his own words, a "treasure trove of common memory." But libraries have passed this first stage in their development: they can no longer acquire and store all or even significant portions of available publications. Even the largest research libraries have entered into cooperative acquisition and interlibrary loan arrangements.

Instead of owning materials, libraries must now make highly selective choices of what they will hold and what they will provide access to. Technology makes access the next important step in library development. By emphasizing access along with its own holdings, the library accomplishes its role of preserving the record of knowledge. Technology makes this possible and it is wonderful. But even the approach of worldwide access, as positive as it is, is still based on the model of knowledge as accumulation of information about parts. As such, it dooms both the student and the library. There is simply too much information. Furthermore, the purpose of usage for the library remains the same: to do research and to gain access to more and more information in order to attain mastery of the enormous amount available on almost any topic.

Access, like holdings, is not a sufficient concept to accommodate fully technology and the knowledge explosion. Libraries have properly developed a third step that focuses on the ability to use the library and its new search and retrieval technologies. We call this skill *information literacy*. This step is an important one that is not given adequate emphasis at most institutions. Information literacy means enabling students to identify information needs, develop search strategies, and analyze information content. At a minimum, information literacy involves the library in providing students bibliographic instruction. At its best, information literacy can and should be integrated into all curricula as one of the learning outcomes of higher education. A few institutions have begun to move in this direction. For example, the Fielding Institute, a doctoral level institution, has identified eight learning outcomes for its information literacy program (Kunkel, 1994):

1. An understanding and appreciation of the importance of information in our society
2. The ability to articulate and focus information needs
3. An understanding of the structure and form of information
4. Recognition of the points of access to information
5. The ability to develop strategies of information gathering

6. The ability to evaluate and analyze information content
7. The ability to synthesize, manage, and report results of an information search
8. The ability to evaluate the information search process

Information literacy skills are grounded in the paradigm of retrieving and mastering information on a topic. They are primarily about managing information and using it as before. As developed more fully later in this chapter, a primary response to the technology revolution and information explosion should be a new understanding of knowing and learning in which technology and information help promote the learning process and the evolving creation of knowledge itself, including the students' (or users') creation of new knowledge through their use of these materials.

**Quantum Physics Model.** Quantum physics presents an entirely new organizing principle of reality that is only beginning to find its way into science, organizational development, and society at large. Quantum physics came about from the study of subatomic particles—in our constant quest to know more and more about less and less—the parts that make up the atom. These parts include electrons, protons, and neutrons, and this study led to ever-smaller sub-sub-atomic parts being identified. To their surprise, scientists learned that these particles can display different properties. An electron can be both a particle and a wave, meaning that it has totally different physical realities. This discovery has led to a new worldview with profound implications (Wheatley, 1993, pp. 9–10). First, something may be both one thing and another thing at the same time (a particle and a wave) but what it is depends on the context in which it is functioning or on how it is being viewed. This leads to a second point: the relationships between parts is as important as the parts themselves. In quantum physics, particles do not exist as independent "things" but come into being and are observed only in relationship to something else. Third, the act of observing or measuring something affects it. As Wheatley describes it, the observer participates in the creation of the very thing he or she is observing or measuring.

**Not "Either-Or" but "And."** What does the quantum physics model mean for higher education and libraries? First, the library needs to be seen both as an independent entity and as a major contributor to the learning process. It is not an either-or proposition. In the quantum physics model, the context for observation is critical; so too is defining the mission of the library and its role in the teaching and learning processes of the institution. The organizing principle used can define not only indicators of quality but the mission and attributes of organization and functioning for the library (and the institution as a whole). The next and fourth stage of development for the library is to serve as a full partner in transforming the act of learning. This is an emerging role and an increasingly critical one. Elements of this new role are already in place at many institutions with changes taking place in the library, the wiring of the campus, the merging of computing and information resources, and the increased technical expertise of library staff. As libraries develop learning outcomes and then apply quality indicators based on their contribution to the learning process, the new role will become better defined and understood. Partnerships between librarians and faculty can accelerate the achievement of the new role. The main point is that the library needs to be taken out of its confining role as a support service and seen as a central element in any institution's response to the learner of the future.

**Seeing the Library in Relationship.** The real value of the library is determined by its relationship to other parts of the whole. In this fourth stage in the development of the library, it functions as a dynamic and primary learning center that can be evaluated by its contributions to student learning and, ultimately, by its contribution to a changing definition of knowledge and learning itself. What relationships are critical in this new model?

*Relationship to the educational mission and goals of the institution.* Every institution's goal is to prepare its students effectively for the twenty-first century. The library, in collaboration with the faculty, should define what contributions to student learning are expected from it. These direct and primary educational goals should become part of a library mission statement. The library certainly has a key role to play in developing information literacy skills. It can also play a role in instilling the habits of lifelong learning. It can develop critical thinking through its own displays and programs as well as through its support for student learning. Technology will play an increasingly important role in the next century and the medium itself is a source of great creativity and learning. As the library adapts to new technology, usually well in advance of classrooms on campus, it becomes an important source of student learning about technology, its limits, uses, and integration into all elements of life. Moreover, to the extent that an institution embraces the goal of self-awareness among students of their own learning styles and habits, the library can play an important role in developing this awareness.

*Relationship to the institutional program review process.* Most institutions have processes for systematic review of all academic and nonacademic departments and units. Such program reviews are often mini-accreditation processes. In many cases, the process is a powerful internal force for self-assessment and program improvement and the best way to engage departmental faculty on issues related to quality and effectiveness. Increasingly, accreditation teams evaluate the effectiveness of the program review process because it is impossible for any visiting team to evaluate each and every program during a visit. In the course of supporting dozens of accrediting teams over the years, I have observed that the library is rarely connected to the program review of academic departments.

Recently, as a special research project, I analyzed the program review criteria of fifteen institutions ranging from selective liberal arts colleges to medium and large comprehensive universities. Many of the criteria were well developed and reflected considerable attention to questions or topics considered important to academic quality. Fourteen of the fifteen institutions did not address in any way the specific issue of information literacy, although it could be raised independently by a department if it were a departmental goal or outcome. One institution had revised its program review process to establish eleven outcomes-oriented criteria. One of the eleven criteria related to technology was the following: "Each program will expose students to technology that is appropriate to their discipline and their needs" (Westmont, 1995, p. 11). Five institutional statements of program review criteria did not mention the word "library" at all, one asked a question about evidence of library usage, and the remaining eight addressed library and technology issues only through such topics as support services, available resources, and quality of holdings.

The findings indicated that the prevailing mode of thinking is that library issues are not directly connected to departmental quality and that the library is perceived to be only a support service.

Such a view is similarly maintained by the otherwise excellent handbook on program review published by the American Association of Colleges and Universities (1992), which addresses program goals, curriculum structure, connected learning, teaching quality, assessment, advising, and other topics. Remarkably, nowhere in the handbook is there mention of information literacy, library assignments, library or research support, or technology and the knowledge explosion as an impetus to develop new models of learning.

Rapid changes make it imperative for faculties to identify how technology and the information explosion are affecting their discipline and the expected learning outcomes of their graduates. Institutions need to examine their program review criteria and consider what assumptions are contained in the statement of criteria. Is the organizing principle based on resources or student learning? Included in the review should also be a clear and substantive relationship with the library that goes beyond the submission of data on the number of holdings in the discipline. For example, syllabi reviews should consider library assignments and the ways in which technology and technology issues are integrated into course work. To what extent do students participate in bibliographic instruction? How does the department, together with the library, prepare students for lifelong learning?

The library itself should be subject to periodic program review apart from the accreditation process. Such a review should also focus on the learning outcomes of the library. What value does the library add to student learning? What evidence is there that such learning is taking place? The library should also use the program review process to assess its relationships to other campus units and the academic departments.

The self-study process should evaluate the effectiveness of the program review process in terms of its engagement with issues surrounding the transformation of the library. Moreover, because the self-study involves leaders from all parts of the institution, it should also assess the effectiveness of the library's relationship to other parts of the campus and its contributions to student learning.

*Relationship to curriculum and course approval processes.* Every campus has a faculty committee or process to review and approve new courses and programs. The library tends to be connected to such processes only indirectly through issues of availability of support resources. This too reflects the organizing principle that resources are the primary indicator of library quality.

Many more substantive issues are involved in relating the library to the curriculum and course approval process. For example, questions should be asked about how course assignments or curricular design promote information literacy. Breivik and Gee demonstrate convincingly (1989) that library-based learning can make important contributions to the learning process and needs to be integrated into curricular planning. With respect to technology issues, curriculum and course reviews should include consideration of whether any new course or program adequately incorporates technology and addresses technology issues. Including such questions in existing institutional processes can have a significant influence. As librarians develop more skills in information technology they are in the perfect position to assist faculty in the development of new course materials and pedagogy (Wolff, 1994, p. 132).

*Relationship to the institution's assessment efforts.* All institutions engage in a variety of assessment efforts, particularly in relation to student learning and institutional effectiveness. Library assessment efforts could be far better coordinated with such institutional assessment efforts, especially those linked to student learning.

How these relationships are assessed is directly related to the fundamental mission of the library. If the library is seen as a support service, one set of questions is relevant. If it is seen as a source of direct learning, then another type of questioning is. As already noted in this chapter, all too often library assessments are geared toward resources, research capacity, and effectiveness of support rather than toward effect on the learning process and the learner. The act of engaging students in assessment can affect them by highlighting the educational goals of the library.

Some examples are useful. As institutions move toward collecting data on usage, will anyone seek to know why students take books out, how they use them, and what they learned about not only the search process but also the process of learning itself? If the library is considered a separate entity, usage statistics alone are enough. They can be very useful to demonstrate the need for more money or more staff or more bibliographic instruction. But such data do not indicate whether students have learned effective information search and retrieval skills, can discriminate between relevant and irrelevant information, or use research techniques to solve problems. Nor will they reveal if students are learning how to create new knowledge or understand an issue for themselves.

Similar problems arise from surveys on how frequently students visit and how much time they spend in the library, which are common questions. User satisfaction surveys also have similar problems. What does "satisfaction" mean? Does it mean satisfaction with the library as a research entity that enabled a user to get a paper done or as a support entity that did some preliminary research? What would happen if the goal of satisfaction surveys was to determine how effectively the library enriched the course or curriculum or educational experience of the student? Or to determine whether library staff had an impact in helping students become lifelong learners?

## Moving the Library to a New Role: Transforming Learning

**Redefining Knowledge.** The metaphor of the shift from Newtonian to quantum physics suggests that learning needs to become far more than mastery of facts. Higher education needs to identify the fundamental skills, capabilities, and attitudes that learners of the future will need. To do so the purposes and ends of the educational process must be reassessed. Technology and the information explosion will affect not only the quantity of information available and our access to it but the very definitions of *knowledge* and *learning*. What we have traditionally viewed as the content of learning will change as fundamentally as the process of learning. What does it mean to prepare students for a future where there will always be more readily accessible information on any topic than can be mastered? And where the content as well as the underlying foundational principles of the disciplines on which it rests may change at least once (if not more often) during an individual lifetime?

The quantum shift in education means moving beyond mastery of facts although facts clearly form a part of the newly emerging model of education. Senge (1990, p. 13) calls this shift *metanoia*, a fundamental shift of mind. Such a shift involves knowledge of interconnectedness and relationships, as well as knowledge of facts, and self-awareness about the learning process itself. Education will need to focus as much on the context in which facts exist as on the facts themselves. The learner of the future will need to be prepared with basic though transcendent skills, be disciplined in the process of learning, and be capable of applying ever-changing information to new situations. The library of the future can play a central role in this process.

**Embracing the Library's New Role.** The library not only provides a link to the vast information resources available but also is already developing new levels of expertise in both access to and generation of knowledge. The fourth stage of library development includes a role as campus leader in the redefinition of knowledge and the transformation of learning. "In-formation" is the character of the knowledge explosion. Libraries are connected both to the subject matter and the emerging technologies for gaining access to it. Far more than an archivist or support worker, the librarian of the future will play a critical role as teacher. A recent Stanford University evaluation of its undergraduate education included a survey of 750 faculty in three schools responsible for undergraduate education. The responses showed that most faculty did not employ technological aids in their courses and most neither exploited existing campus resources on technology nor were able to evaluate the effectiveness of such technology (Stanford, 1994, p. 39). Students of all ages coming to our institutions have technological skills equal or superior to those of most of the faculty. Library staff, in coordination with others, can play a leading role not only in helping faculty understand how to access information (gain information literacy) but also in working with faculty to integrate technology and new information resources into the curriculum. As already suggested, this ability will be the education of the future as much as the content of any course.

Furthermore, the new mode of learning can become truly generative—learning that enhances the capacity to create—with the assistance of technology and information resources combined with library-based assignments. Thus, I propose that libraries redefine their missions to encompass serving as an archive and access provider and as lead teacher to the institution about transforming learning. Future planning and assessment activities at the institutional level (as well as in the library itself) need to address the changing character of knowledge and learning, the fundamental interconnectedness of learning technology, information literacy, and the student of the future. Such conversations need to be at the center of planning and assessment efforts, not on the periphery. Librarians can and should be centrally involved in these discussions and even have the ability to lead them.

## New Partnerships Between Librarians and Faculty

Librarians alone cannot forge their new roles. Nor can they wave a magic wand and include these kinds of issues in institutional planning, curriculum approval, or program review processes. Instead, they may take several approaches:

*Use existing faculty and library committees.* Many libraries have faculty liaison committees and library staff often serve on standing faculty committees. These ideas should be raised and explored in these committees. Special coalitions should be developed with members of the faculty interested in the integration of technology, learning issues, pedagogy, and curriculum development. Wherever possible, the senior administration's support, encouragement, and leadership are important; efforts need to be taken to develop a shared vision.

*Collaborate with faculty in scholarship efforts.* Librarians should attempt to collaborate with faculty members interested in the scholarship of application and pedagogy and work to publish together conceptual models for new approaches to learning and the interconnectedness of the library in discipline-based journals. These issues need to be moved out of the inner world of librarianship to the broader academic community through such collaborative work.

*Participate in and lead faculty development efforts.* Across the country, greater attention is being placed on teaching effectiveness. Many campuses have already established centers to support the improvement of faculty teaching. Librarians should be actively involved in such activities and lead singly or collaboratively faculty workshops on these topics.

*Participate in faculty evaluation efforts.* Along with faculty development, efforts are under way to change the ways in which faculty effectiveness is evaluated. Student evaluation forms are being revised, faculty portfolios developed, and peer reviews strengthened. Librarians need to form partnerships so that these processes include review of issues relating to technology and information resources and the changing character of the learning process.

## Conclusion

The Newtonian model of separating the world into independent parts is reaching the end of its usefulness in both higher education and the larger society. The quantum physics model outlines a new approach built around relationships and multiple roles and gives form to the fundamentally changing character of knowledge and the learning process. The mission of the library of the future will be principally a teaching one that is directly linked to the educational mission of the institution. Thus, assessment should be directed primarily at the library's relationship to the teaching and learning functions of the institution. Any evaluation should emphasize how interaction with the library affects or enhances student learning. Through the self-study and visit processes, accreditation can play a useful role in exploring each of these issues and promoting the development of new partnerships throughout the institution.

## References

American Association of Colleges and Universities. *Program Review and Educational Quality in the Major: A Faculty Handbook.* Washington, D.C.: American Association of Colleges and Universities, 1992.
Appleberry, J. B. "Changes in Our Future: How Will We Cope?" Speech presented at California State University, Long Beach, Aug. 28, 1992.
Breivik, P. S., and Gee, E. G. *Information Literacy: Revolution in the Library.* New York: American Council on Education/Macmillan, 1989.
Coleman, P., and Jarred, A. D. "Regional Association Criteria and the Standards for College Libraries: The Informal Role of Quantitative Input Measures for Libraries in Accreditation." *Journal of Academic Librarianship,* Nov. 1994, pp. 273–284.
Garten, E. D. "Current Regional Commission Standards and Guidelines." In E. Garten (ed.), *The Challenge and Practice of Academic Accreditation: A Sourcebook for Library Administrators.* Westport, Conn.: Greenwood Press, 1994.
Kuhn, T. S. *The Structure of Scientific Revolutions.* Chicago: University of Chicago Press, 1970.
Kunkel, L. K. *Information Literacy: Basic Competencies.* Santa Barbara, Calif.: Fielding Institute, 1994.
Leach, R. "Academic Library Change: The Role of Regional Accreditation." *Journal of Academic Librarianship,* 1992, *18* (5) 288–291.
Martell, C. Presentation at the Western Association of Schools and Colleges Presidents' Forum, Nov. 6, 1991.
Middle States Association of Colleges and Schools. *Characteristics of Excellence in Higher Education.* Philadelphia: Middle States Association of Colleges and Schools, 1992.
Pelikan, J. *The Idea of the University: A Reexamination.* New Haven, Conn.: Yale University Press, 1992.
Reich, R. B. *The Work of Nations: Preparing Ourselves for 21st-Century Capitalism.* New York: Vintage Books, 1992.
Senge, P. M. *The Fifth Discipline: The Art and Practice of the Learning Organization.* New York: Doubleday, 1990.
Stanford University. *Report of the Commission on Undergraduate Education.* Palo Alto, Calif.: Stanford University, 1994.

Westmont College. *Standards for Program Quality and Evidence of Excellence.* Santa Barbara, Calif.: Westmont College, 1995.

Wheatley, M. J. *Leadership and the New Science: Learning About Organization from an Orderly Universe.* San Francisco: Berrett-Koehler, 1993.

Wolff, R. "Rethinking the Librarian's Role on Accrediting Teams." *C&RL News,* 1992, *53,* 450–451.

Wolff, R. "Rethinking Library Self-Studies and Accreditation Visits." In E. Garten (ed.), *The Challenge and Practice of Academic Accreditation: A Sourcebook for Library Administrators.* Westport, Conn.: Greenwood Press, 1994.

Wolff, R., and Steadman, M. H. "Accreditation Expectations in the Age of New Technology." In E. Garten (ed.), *The Challenge and Practice of Academic Accreditation: A Sourcebook for Library Administrators.* Westport, Conn.: Greenwood Press, 1994.

*RALPH A. WOLFF is associate executive director of the accrediting commission for senior colleges and universities of the Western Association of Schools and Colleges and founder of the Institute for Creative Thinking.*

*Technology's role in defining the future of libraries will be shaped by the broader changes that its advances are now contributing to the evolution of higher education institutions and the systems of scholarly communication.*

# The Technological Framework for Library Planning in the Next Decade

*Clifford A. Lynch*

From the popular rhetoric about digital libraries, virtual libraries, universities without physical library facilities, and similar topics it seems clear that the expectation in some quarters is that technology will fundamentally change the nature of the university research library by the end of the twentieth century. This chapter suggests not that these predictions are intrinsically wrong but rather that they proceed from an increasingly less relevant and useful set of assumptions.

There is growing evidence that the higher education system in the United States will be subjected to enormous and wrenching changes over the next decade as a result of the convergence of a variety of technological developments and economic, political, and demographic trends. One can take a broad policy perspective on these trends and the ways in which they will change the university system—as a university president or other senior administrator might—considering issues such as the changing demographics of the student body or the erosion of public support for higher education. Or one can view the changing environment from within the context of one of the scholarly disciplines that the university system has historically supported and think in terms of changes in the processes of teaching, learning, research, and scholarly communication. Such a view might reflect more accurately that of a faculty member in today's university. Whichever vantage point one chooses, however, it seems clear that significant changes are in the offing.

To understand fully the technological framework in which research library roles will develop it is necessary to examine the broader forces shaping the university as an institution as well as those that are altering the nature of the scholarly disciplines. This chapter explores how technology is changing university

NEW DIRECTIONS FOR HIGHER EDUCATION, no. 90, Summer 1995 © Jossey-Bass Publishers

programs and missions, how the nature of the university community (and particularly the students within it) is shifting, and how the scholarly communication system is being reshaped. These are the forces that define the technological framework for libraries in the 1990s and beyond.

This brief chapter tries to place technology-driven changes in university libraries over the next decade in the broader context of changes in higher education programs and missions and that of the impact of greater access to information technology. Although technology may make certain new library services possible these services may not make sense within the context of the changing nature of higher education and its client base. Some of the possible new services may well not be implemented. In contrast, some of the new library services mandated by the changing university environment will be hard to provide even with advances in technology, in part because there will be little or no precedent in how to design or deploy them. Yet, whatever the difficulties, many of these services are likely to be implemented simply because they are important to the institution and the patron community.

## The End of Technological Determinism in Library Planning

A fundamental fallacy underlies much of the recent discussion about planning for the future of university research libraries. No doubt technology is creating exciting new opportunities for them to reconsider the means through which they implement their basic missions to select and acquire, organize, provide access to, and preserve, information of all types. But the evolution of research libraries as they enter the networked information age will not be determined by technological opportunities alone. It must and increasingly will be guided by the priorities of their host higher educational institutions, and will not be defined by technology as it relates to research libraries as independent institutions. University research libraries will not become "virtual libraries" or "digital libraries" simply because doing so is or will soon be possible; evolution determined merely by technology-enabled possibilities is a luxury we can no longer afford.

Visions of the library of the future outside of the broader context of the changing nature of the university are likely to be seriously misinformed. Priorities for the implementation of technological opportunities will be defined by institutional economic priorities on the one hand (for example, the need to convert parts of collections to digital formats in order to avoid building new libraries) and institutional programmatic initiatives on the other (the need to provide electronic information resources that can support institutional commitments to instructional technology and distance education).

The 1970s and 1980s were good years for library administrations, at least for strategic planning and the introduction of information technology. Although the budgetary picture varied yearly (and in the later part of the period most budgets declined in terms of real purchasing power and certainly in terms of ability to acquire relative to the overall volume of published literature), the world remained relatively stable from a programmatic perspective. Collection development ebbed and flowed based on academic programs and budgets. Through the early 1980s the typical pattern was one of growth, reflecting the expansion of academic programs. During the later 1980s and early 1990s retrenchment occurred across the entire range of acquisitions priorities as budget pressures became severe.

But there was still a sense that the library understood its priorities and its destiny. The period was also characterized by extensive deployment of information technology to streamline and improve existing library operations and services. The introduction of automated circulation systems and shared copy cataloging on a national and international basis provided substantial cost savings and efficiency improvements. On-line catalogs and electronic access to abstracting and indexing data bases through on-line services or CD-ROM technology represented important incremental improvements in the quality of service offered.

The nature of the host institutions remained relatively constant during this period and libraries mapped their own evolution based on their internal priorities. There was a sense of predictability in the planning process and the development of visions for the library of the future. The central issue was how to make the library more effective in meeting what was fundamentally a well-understood and well-defined mission. Although some technology-based developments, such as access to on-line catalogs and other electronic services through the Internet, supported changing university academic programs and the user community by facilitating access from outside the library on a twenty-four-hour-a-day basis, it is striking to note the extent to which these were an almost accidental consequence of deploying systems intended to improve traditional library services rather than an application of technology targeted to achieve these goals.

I suspect that libraries will have increasingly less latitude in the coming years to pursue autonomously defined, technologically determined manifest destiny at a pace that is comfortable to the library administration and staff (and patrons), and hope that this future will conveniently and serendipitously converge with university programmatic needs. Instead, libraries will be expected to provide leadership in supporting institutional programmatic objectives and to move more rapidly than they have in the past.

To date, the library's progress toward its own self-defined technological destiny often has been characterized more by intense, occasionally self-congratulatory discussion than by rapid and aggressive action. It should be recognized that libraries by and large have been conservative (often, to be fair, justifiably and wisely so); their positions with regard to the massive changes beginning to transfigure the system of scholarly communication and the marketplace for electronic information have been largely characterized by caution, skepticism, occasional denial, and some resistance. They have raised legitimate questions about whether the high acquisition and delivery costs of the new electronic information resources are justified in comparison to more traditional materials. In developing strategies to respond to the changing nature of the higher education environment they have frequently made common cause with equally conservative and skeptical faculty—properly viewing these faculty as the single most critical constituency they serve. As a result they have often chosen to move cautiously in a support role to the faculty rather than to lead the way in exploiting the opportunities offered by the networked information environment and, indeed, in moving the overall university community toward the new environment.

## The University in the Networked Information Age

Although the rate of change has been a problem, the objectives of change have been a greater one. Libraries have tended to emphasize objectives that simply extrapolate from traditional service offerings rather than from new university programmatic strategies or new modes of societal discourse and scholarly communication; this is in part because of the difficulty in understanding these new programmatic strategies and the environment in which they are being defined. These programmatic strategies are only now beginning to be clearly articulated by university administrations and scholars. Scholarly societies are struggling to characterize the changing nature of communication within their communities.

As institutions, universities are having a great deal of trouble charting their directions. It is clear that the world they function in is changing and that they must change along with it. It seems likely that the new world will be a more competitive one and that although the most prestigious traditional research universities, the great historic institutions like Harvard, MIT, and the University of California, Berkeley, will have the option of surviving for quite some time with relatively little change, the survival of many other institutions is at issue. Furthermore, at least some of the finest of the research institutions have maintained their status by periodic reinvention. The changing environment will challenge them to reinvent themselves again. The institutions that will remain great will not only survive in the new world but also treat the transition as an opportunity to transform themselves.

Universities—particularly public institutions—are beginning to serve new and different constituencies. Information technology is making it possible for them to reach communities of learners independent of schedule and geography; a nationally renowned department within a university will soon be able to project its educational and research "products" worldwide. These products will compete on a national and ultimately a global basis with other institutions' offerings through distance education technologies; universities will at the same time cooperate to further the development of knowledge within scholarly communities and compete with one another in the delivery of instruction and the conduct of research far more directly than they have in the past. As these educational offerings reach new audiences (potentially global in scope), the nature of both the student body and the community of participating scholars will change as will the expectations about support services like libraries.

In the marketplace for educational services that we are likely to see in the early twenty-first century, where geography is much less of a factor than it once was, it cannot simply be assumed that the current population of full-service universities will survive. It will be much easier for the institutions delivering the highest quality instruction and conducting the highest quality research to dominate the marketplace for education. Institutional responses will include alliances and consortia and even consolidation in their quest to retain competitive levels of quality at competitive costs. We may see the formation of constellations of local centers of learning that function primarily as support vehicles and access points for a limited number of primary institutions that deliver very high-quality distance education. Also, for professional and job-oriented instruction, there will be growing competition from nontraditional (even for-profit) corporate-based education, which will be committed to instructional technologies of all kinds, will be less burdened with tradition than will traditional institutions, and will be well supplied with investment funds to explore new technological opportunities.

As distance education programs and instructional technologies become greater priorities, libraries will be expected to provide a new range of support services. The services will include not only distance access to information resources in general and to specific types of information that directly support instruction (for example, electronic reserve collections) but also provision of faculty support for the construction of multimedia courseware.

Disciplines of study now in danger of falling below critical mass at any single institution because of their specialized nature and limited communities may be rejuvenated as they cross institutional boundaries through distance learning technologies, collaborative research, and learning environments based on computer communications networking. Library services will be needed in these new environments but they will be very different services from those traditionally provided to patrons visiting libraries in person. We do not understand the nature of these new library services well (nor, indeed, the character of the new computer-based environments they will need to support). The library services will clearly emphasize digital content and network-based delivery of material (whether originating in digital form or printed formats) but also emphasize integration of content with collaboration tools.

Recorded lectures and other interactions (including recordings of use of the collaboration environments, group project work, problem sessions, and the like) and instructional courseware will also be important content to support these new environments and will expand the library's role to that of knowledge manager and manager of direct instructional materials as well as of traditional published literature that supports instruction and research.

Large-scale deployment and exploitation of computer communications networks represents the death knell of geography as a defining principle of client groups for both commercial enterprises and organizations such as universities and their libraries. The end of geography will require not only new technology-based services but also new policies on interlibrary cooperation and the definition of user communities and perhaps new assumptions about funding sources and even governance.

## The Changing University Community

A second fallacy that underlies much of the current planning for the future of research libraries also stems from a failure to recognize the changing nature of the library's context. Just as the library must support new programmatic initiatives of the host educational institution, it must support the changing nature of its user community. Research libraries have been unwilling to assume that their user communities have almost ubiquitous access to information technologies such as personal computers and network connections, even as they design their new service offerings. They have shared this ambivalence about the availability of technology to the user community with university administrations, which have agonized long and hard over issues such as whether (or perhaps more accurately, how soon) they can require students and faculty at the institution to own personal computers and utilize them for routine access to infrastructure services such as electronic mail. These reservations are based on honest, deeply felt concerns about equity of access and equity of opportunity.

But the nature of the user base (both students and faculty) is in fact changing. Most library users do have access to computers and increasingly also to networks, and this majority continues to grow. Library users are exploiting this base of information technology to gain productivity in their business and personal lives. They are less willing to be denied similar benefits in their educational experiences. The new user community is ever less sympathetic to being held hostage by a "trailing edge" of users who are unwilling to invest in appropriate information technology and the skills needed to use it effectively. This impatience applies to faculty who have resisted the adoption of information technology; the university community of the future will be no more inclined to tolerate faculty who cannot communicate through electronic mail or make their course reserve materials available for electronic access than it is to tolerate those who refuse to acquire or learn to use telephones today. Although there is a recognition that some students and even faculty may be willing to embrace the new communications technologies but simply face economic barriers in doing so, there is growing pressure to move beyond recognizing this state of affairs to devising some means of addressing it.

These impatient individuals have learned, often through experience in the business world, to value their own time and demand respect as participants in the academic life of the institution. They will not tolerate bad service and interminable lines for registration; they will not tolerate libraries that are closed when they need to do their homework or research; they will not tolerate faculty who refuse to communicate with them.

Among the faculty, a new generation who were raised with information technology and a rich array of electronic information resources as graduate students are rising to prominence. They look to the networked information environment not only as a medium within which they expect to receive library services but also as a medium in which instruction and research is facilitated. Increasingly they will be the stronger voices in demanding new information services that support instruction and research, and they will expect these services to be smoothly integrated into their own working and learning environments. Libraries will be expected to understand and accommodate these new learning and research environments rather than to design library services that stand alone.

As network users, both the new students and new faculty view information access as a marketplace. They are growing accustomed to using information wherever it is available and selecting the best and most convenient information suppliers from the competitive information marketplace of the net. Unconstrained by geography, a growing number of information providers will compete for their attention and their business. As consumers, this new community will seek to establish financial models that empower them to choose among potential suppliers. If their institutional library is not a presence on the net, or provides inappropriate services or limited content, other for-profit or nonprofit information providers (including, for example, scholarly and professional societies) will quickly rise to the opportunity. And the network environment will permit research libraries to compete with each other for users; if increased financial decision-making responsibility moves to the individual student or faculty member (as will be the case if fee-for-service access to materials becomes more commonplace), this competition could become intense.

Many questions about technical strategies in the new environment are unresolved. Until now, libraries have tended to focus on delivering services based on comprehensive end-to-end models: the library deploys a system that includes content, retrieval tools, and a user interface. In the near future, the library may be called upon instead to provide content and limited retrieval tools that can interoperate with a variety of commercial or public domain user interfaces and information management and analysis software packages that will be selected and acquired directly by members of the user community. This software, which may include automated information seeking and acquisition programs that operate continuously and relatively autonomously (various types of software "agents" or "knowbots"), will work cooperatively with the library retrieval software to identify and select information of interest to the patron and move it to the patron's machine for analysis, storage, and integration with information that the patron already has or has obtained from other network-based information providers.

This is a very different type of environment for the library; its services may become less well defined in identity to the patron and appear to be more of a commodity. Its services will be increasingly unusable unless the patron has access to sophisticated information technology and does not come to the library to use them but rather subscribes to them across the network. There will be an emphasis on information that can be readily reused, repackaged, and reorganized. The design of library services in this environment will be driven by an emphasis on standards and broad inter-operability.

Consider the distance between this near-future technological environment and the current one. The emphasis in the development or acquisition of library systems to date has been on a complete system that delivers service directly to patrons sitting in the library and, almost like an afterthought, may also provide remote access from a limited set of workstation platforms, perhaps even requiring the patron who wishes such access to install special software that the library provides. In the future, convenient access by the machines owned by the user community (and by software systems resident on those machines) will be the dominant criterion in the design and selection of library automation systems.

The implications of a shift in the focus of delivery to end-user machines will have other pervasive effects on the information technology infrastructure in universities, including the library. Within the next few years, classrooms, laboratories, offices, and libraries will be expected to provide convenient connectivity (both wired and wireless) for portable machines that are carried from place to place. The number of public access workstations in the library will diminish, just as public-access workstation rooms will become less of an issue in the university as a whole. Public access machines will be available as conveniences, much as pay telephones are conveniences rather than replacements for personal telephones today. Instead of the banks of public access terminals or workstations now found in libraries that have invested in electronic information resources, we will see large numbers of docking facilities for personal machines that provide electrical and network connections.

In this vision of the future, the new user community will find that many of the systems now used by libraries to provide access to electronic information are inappropriate and unresponsive. Closed systems of all types that do not offer flexible, standards-based network access will be unacceptable, including many turnkey on-line catalogs, remote systems that can be accessed only at terminals in the library, and particularly stand-alone CD-ROM systems. Yet many of today's systems continue to exist, primarily because the content providers are unwilling to lose control over their content by offering the sort of flexible standards-based network access facilities that the new user community will eventually demand. As they plan their migration to the new technical framework, libraries will have to educate and negotiate with the content providers and work with university information technology and networking infrastructure technology developers to establish access control and authentication systems that will allow them to complete successful negotiations with these content providers.

## Libraries and the Systems of Scholarly Communication

University research libraries serve two masters: the scholarly disciplines of the university faculty and the programmatic objectives of the university administrations. This chapter focuses on how institutional changes will shape library services. But the scholarly disciplines are also being transformed by changes in the systems of scholarly communication (which vary widely among disciplines). These changes raise fundamental questions for libraries.

Scholarly publishing is a means to an end; its original purpose was to support and maintain scholarly communication for successive generations of scholars and students. The system of scholarly publishing involves authors, readers, and publishers (commercial publishers as well as nonprofit publishers such as university presses and professional and scholarly societies). Libraries are also an integral part of scholarly publishing. For a number of reasons, this system is under intense economic pressure. The authors and readers whom the system serves are finding it increasingly unresponsive to many of their needs. The publication process is too slow in some disciplines, and finding a publication venue in which to communicate with one's colleagues is a long and frustrating process. The economic and technological restrictions of print technology, such as page limits or the inability to include computer programs, interactive graphics, or large data sets as part of a paper, also inhibit the ability of some authors to communicate with their peers as effectively and as richly as they might wish. Publishers can place restrictions on the free flow of information within the community and its use in teaching and research that authors and readers find infuriating and counterproductive. Costs of published works in some disciplines have become extraordinarily expensive, creating another barrier to access.

As a result of these concerns, experimentation with new forms of scholarly communication is occurring. In one new model, the authors themselves function as the publishers. I believe, however, that this model has severe management and scaling problems. A third party or parties that combine elements of the traditional roles of publishers and libraries in the traditional print publishing environment—particularly the roles of maintaining communications for archival purposes and of organizing the products of many authors to allow readers to locate and obtain materials—will eventually be needed. The extent to which university libraries, as opposed to professional and scholarly societies or other organizations, will fulfill these requirements is as yet unknown. In a networked environment, where geography is not a significant organizing factor, management of scholarly communication may be distributed along disciplinary lines, favoring the professional and scholarly societies. It may, however, be distributed based on authors' organizational affiliations, favoring the university libraries. The latter scenario would represent a much more challenging situation because many distributed, autonomous libraries would have to cooperate to provide scholars with a coherent view of a disciplinary literature. Current economic models tend to favor libraries in the lead role, although nothing would prevent libraries from funding scholarly and professional societies or other organizations to do the actual work.

The ramifications of this new model for library technology planning are extensive. In essence, this model requires that libraries be able to acquire complex multimedia content from authors, organize this content as part of an international system, provide access to the content, and ensure the ongoing preservation of access to the content (which is particularly difficult for multimedia electronic resources). They will also need to integrate this content into the new delivery systems and contexts (described earlier in this chapter) that are being dictated by changing institutional needs. Successfully undertaking these roles may be essential if research libraries are to continue to effectively serve the scholarly disciplines. Libraries will be challenged to understand and remain current with the technologies of communication and publication being used by the various disciplines and to persuade authors and readers within these disciplines that libraries have value to add to the process and possess the technical competence to effectively add that value.

There are other models of scholarly communication under discussion that propose removing the university libraries from the process. Materials would be made available directly to readers by publishers, and the publishers (either commercial or nonprofit) would also fill some of the archival and organizing functions that the library has traditionally served. In this model, the role of the library is relegated to paying much of the bill through some form of subsidy, at least until control of the funds is moved back from the library to the readers.

Interestingly, in some cases the publisher in this model is being termed an electronic library. If examples of this model come to fruition, there will still be technological implications for libraries, since the contents of these repositories will still need to be integrated in some fashion with other materials that the university libraries continue to hold and offer access to directly. And, although the model of publisher disintermediation described above is already moving into wide operation, in part because it can be implemented on a distributed, grass-roots basis by authors, the model of library disintermediation in favor of national or international disciplinary libraries requires the adoption of a plan by an entire community.

With respect to changing systems of scholarly communication, the library's mission will be to bridge across and provide coherent organization and access to an increasingly diverse set of communications systems. I do not believe that the current system of scholarly publishing will cease to exist in the near future, although it may diminish somewhat in volume, and there is little question that it will be supplemented by a range of other models. Authors are independent individuals and will choose different venues to communicate with their peers. In addition, even if disciplinary culture and sociology produce a reasonably homogeneous model of communication within a given discipline, the growing emphasis on multidisciplinary studies will only underscore the need for libraries to provide some coherence across a diversity of disciplinary cultures.

## Raw Materials of Research and Scholarship

One of the most exciting prospects of the networked information environment is its ability to open up access to all types of special collections—photographs, archives, and museum collections—that have been relatively inaccessible to the scholarly community. Electronic surrogates of these materials can be made available not just to the few select scholars who are able to visit a location where the materials are held and invest the time to learn how to handle them, but to any student. This possibility is likely to lead to a renewed emphasis on primary source materials in instruction and research, and to demand on libraries to make these types of materials available in digital forms. Many research libraries have already initiated such programs. The technologies and tools necessary to support these programs are increasingly well understood, although such digitization programs are costly and funding sources are few. It seems clear, however, that this class of projects, which is consistent with the changing environment of the research library described earlier in this chapter, will continue to grow.

A second type of raw material that will be needed to support scholarship today and in the future is access to the content presented through current mass media, particularly television and radio, which falls outside the print publication world on which research libraries traditionally have based their collections. It will be essential that libraries devote attention both to acquisition strategies for obtaining these materials and to technology strategies for organizing and providing access to them. Indexing and delivery of audio and particularly video materials represent a major and relatively unexplored challenge that must be part of the technology planning for research libraries as they enter the twenty-first century. It also should be recognized that if libraries are to serve as custodians for content created by university distance education and instructional technology programs, many of these same technologies will be required to effectively manage the university's own content.

## Conclusion

This chapter has mapped some of the key trends that will define the technological framework for libraries in the next decade and beyond. It has argued that much of this framework will be imposed by external developments rather than evolve from technology as applied to current library services without regard to their changing context. I did not discuss what I believe to be fairly clear extensions of existing library operations to exploit opportunities created by increasingly ubiquitous networking and that have clear service or economic advantages. Examples include the use of electronic data interchange for ordering and paying for library materials and the direct acquisition of electronic content from traditional publishers using the network. These developments will not be simple to implement, particularly when one considers the number of suppliers with which a typical large research library interacts, but at least the objectives are fairly clear.

One theme that has not been explored in this chapter is the increasing focus on control of intellectual property, which is not a direct determinant of the library's technological framework that I have discussed here. It will, however, be a pervasive influence on the design of library services in the networked information environment and will be a primary topic of community debate as universities increase their commitment to approaches such as distance education and instructional technology, and as faculty teaching activities in addition to faculty publications become reusable and resalable properties. Intellectual property rights in the networked environment (which will largely determine the library's ability to offer material electronically) are a subject of much uncertainty and heated debate, and may also be the object of legislative attention in the near future. The issues of this topic go far beyond the scholarly community and involve not only publishing but also film, video, music, and software industries. Resolution of the questions of economics and control may be a deciding factor in some of the restructuring of scholarly communications. Perhaps the major conclusion that can be drawn regarding the library's technological framework is that libraries will become increasingly involved in the management and licensing of intellectual property rights for materials. As the electronic information environment scales up, it will be increasingly necessary to replace specifically negotiated contractual agreements to license materials with automated rights management and clearance systems so that an extensive marketplace in electronic materials can develop. Libraries must be prepared to use these systems as they develop.

There is a real danger in permitting external forces to shape the technological framework for research library planning; however, I believe that in the increasingly competitive and resource-constrained environment of the current university, this is inevitable. It also is important to remember that research libraries have the important societal mission of preserving both the record of scholarship and the raw materials for future scholarship. This mission gives rise to potential projects that have low payoff in the context of parent institutional or disciplinary priorities but that will be important in the long run— for instance, preserving a reasonable amount of the incunabula of the new digital age.

There may be fewer research libraries in the future, just as there may be fewer research universities. Consider the strategy that many libraries have proposed to deal with their increased inability to acquire new materials due to budgetary constraints: access versus ownership, with heavy use of information technology to make access an effective substitute for local collections. Although this strategy can be effective and responsive, it implies that some libraries must continue to collect materials in order to supply them to the libraries that have chosen the access model.

The technological context proposed here is not intended to suggest that research libraries should abandon their traditional missions of selecting, organizing, providing access to, and preserving materials. These missions continue to be vital, and determining how to effectively perform them in a new environment that is technology intensive and rich in electronic information content is a great challenge. But the definition of strategies and tactics to perform these missions will be more substantially shaped by the broader needs of the scholarly disciplines and the higher education system that support research libraries in the coming decade than perhaps they have been in the past.

*CLIFFORD A. LYNCH is director of library automation in the Office of the President, University of California.*

# INDEX

Academic administrative leaders, 25, 28
Academic support managers, 25–26
Accreditation: collection of evidence for, 79–81; organizing principles for, 78–79, 80 (table); traditional standards of, 78, 82; as vehicle for change, 77–78
Administrators: allocation of resources to research by, 37–38; extrainstitutional scrutiny of, 21; political role of, 23–26; preparations for 21st century, 27–28; restructuring of libraries by, 40; and transition to teaching library, 73–74
Adult education, 7, 8
African Americans, education of, 6
American Association of Colleges and Universities, 86
American Council of Education, 24
American Library Association, 64
American Physics Society, 51, 57
Appleberry, J. B., 82
Association of American Publishers, 54
Association of American Universities (AAU), 50, 60
Association of Research Libraries, 50, 57
Atkinson, R., 3, 46
Attention, economics of, 44–45, 61
Audiovisual sources, 103

Baldridge, J. V., 23
Bayma, T., 36
Bibliographic instruction programs, 3
Bibliothèque Nationale (Paris, France), 34
Biology, research methods of, 36
Borman, H., 61
Boyer, E. L., 24
Bradley University, 66
Breivik, P. S., 73–74, 87
Bureaucracy, and electronic publishing, 58–59
Bureaucratic model of university, 23
Business: educational programs of, 9, 97; inroads on academic culture, 22; partnership with universities, 15

Campus academic administrators, 24–25, 27–28
Case Western Reserve University, 66
*Chemical Abstracts*, 36

Chemistry, research methods of, 36
*Chronicle of Higher Education*, 24
Civil rights movement, 6
Clarke, R., 44
Classroom, electronic, 68, 69, 73
Cleveland State University, 66
Client-server environment, 16–17, 51, 55–56, 58, 59–60
Coalition for Networked Information Working Group on Teaching and Learning, 66–67
Coates, J., 34
Coleman, P., 78
"Collaboratory," 44
Collections, research: and academic restructuring, 40; accessibility of, 43, 56, 60, 71, 83; allocation of resources to, 38; audiovisual materials in, 103; conversion to microform, 39; cooperative development of, 48–50, 51, 83; de-emphasizing by teaching libraries, 74; digitization of, 34, 35, 38–39, 40, 53–54, 71, 103; dual-collection adjustment in, 52–53; and economics of publishing, 47–48, 49, 50; focusing of research by, 44–45, 46–47, 61; local imperative of, 49–50, 51; location of, 34–35; on-line, 51–61, 102–103; organization of, 43–44; preservation of original sources in, 39, 40; relative prestige of, 57; retention decisions by, 50–51, 59, 60–61; screening of, 45–46, 59–60; selection of materials for, 46, 47, 53–54, 71; traditional, 45–51, 83; types of sources in, 46–47
College. *See* Administrators; Faculty; Higher education; Instructional programs; Students; University
Collegiate model of university, 23–24, 26
Columbian World Exposition (1893), 69
Commercial model of electronic publishing, 55, 56, 57, 59
Computer centers, academic, 24–25, 38. *See also* Electronic reserve collections; Electronic text centers
Computer mediated communication (CMC), 36–37
Computers. *See* Collections, research, digitization of; Collections, research,

107

# Ordering Information

NEW DIRECTIONS FOR HIGHER EDUCATION is a series of paperback books that provides timely information and authoritative advice about major issues and administrative problems confronting every institution. Books in the series are published quarterly in Spring, Summer, Fall, and Winter and are available for purchase by subscription and individually.

SUBSCRIPTIONS for 1995 cost $48.00 for individuals (a savings of 25 percent over single-copy prices) and $64.00 for institutions, agencies, and libraries. Please do not send institutional checks for personal subscriptions. Standing orders are accepted.

SINGLE COPIES cost $16.95 when payment accompanies order. (California, New Jersey, New York, and Washington, D.C., residents please include appropriate sales tax.) All orders will be charged shipping and handling.

DISCOUNTS FOR QUANTITY ORDERS are available. Please write to the address below for information.

ALL ORDERS must include either the name of an individual or an official purchase order number. Please submit your order as follows:
  *Subscriptions:* specify series and year subscription is to begin
  *Single copies:* include individual title code (such as HE82)

MAIL ALL ORDERS TO:
  Jossey-Bass Publishers
  350 Sansome Street
  San Francisco, California 94104-1342

FOR SUBSCRIPTION SALES OUTSIDE OF THE UNITED STATES, contact any international subscription agency or Jossey-Bass directly.

OTHER TITLES AVAILABLE IN THE
NEW DIRECTIONS FOR HIGHER EDUCATION SERIES
*Martin Kramer,* Editor-in-Chief